Praise for *Why Meditate? Because it Works.*

'Meditation has been life changing for me – I'm so glad I invested the time in learning how to meditate properly. I love working with Jillian because she understands how to fit meditation into our busy lives in a way that's enjoyable and easy. Without a doubt, meditation is the best way to change my mood and help me cope with stress.'

Amelia Freer, nutritional therapist and international best-selling author

'I learnt to meditate with Jillian at a very stressful point in my life (they say that meditation finds you when you need it most). Her meditation practice is backed up by years of research and knowledge: from the way she explains how our brains work; about what exactly happens when we meditate; about its effect not just on our minds, but our bodies and every aspect of our lives from work, to creativity, to energy, and relationships. It's the only type of meditation I could stick to, where everything falls away. It's like sprinkling magic dust over your life.'

Susannah Taylor, wellbeing journalist and columnist at YOU magazine

'The best book about meditation I've come across. Jillian cuts through the noise around what meditation is with clarity and authenticity. We know the devastating toll stress is having on our health. Understanding the power of meditation as a tool for combatting this is invaluable.'

Dr Frank Lipman, functional medicine expert and *New York Times* best-selling author

'I can't imagine life without meditation. My husband and I have been meditating since 1991 and it has supported the best of who I am and how I am. Meditation is spiritual and enlightening, as well as practical and grounding. My three kids meditate, too. I say the family that meditates together stays together.'

Renee Elliot, founder of Planet Organic and co-founder of Beluga Bean

'Meditation allows me to live a fuller and more present life. It helps me sleep better – I fall asleep easier and stay asleep through the night. Jillian makes meditation manageable in a practical, judgment-free way. She's so calm and serene you want to know what her secret is – luckily for us, she teaches it for a living!'

Madeleine Shaw, nutritional therapist and author

'The physical and mental benefits of meditation are well founded but I think the brilliance of Jillian is how she makes this powerful, transformative practice so much more accessible and enjoyable for those who use her methods. I loved having her on my podcast where she spoke with a deep knowledge about the fascinating science behind meditation and shared her own journey to discovering the ancient practice.'

Dr Linda Papadopoulos, psychologist and author

'It's no exaggeration to say learning to meditate changed my life. I've lived with anxiety for as long as I can remember, but I'm better equipped to cope with it since I completed my Vedic Meditation course four years ago. It helps me tune into my body and be more compassionate with myself, my loved ones and my community. This book will demystify the misconceptions you might have about meditation and make you actually want to meditate! When we live in a world that tells us to be anywhere but the present, that is pretty amazing.'

Venetia La Manna, podcaster and fair fashion campaigner

'I'm so pleased Jillian is sharing her life-changing wisdom with the world. What we all need right now is meditation.'

Robert Hammond, co-founder of High Line, New York City

'Meditation has improved my life exponentially, in far too many ways than there is room to list here. The most noticeable life changers have come from simply sitting down, twice a day and letting go of trying, controlling and doing and just allowing things to happen as they are around me. I'm a much more chilled-out, less tense person now, at home, at work and around a dinner table. Plus, I'm not constantly tired. That is a life-changer in itself!'

Suzanne Duckett, journalist, broadcaster and founder of Onolla

'In this straightforward book Jillian lays out what meditation is in mumbo-jumbo free language. There's nothing arcane or esoteric here: Vedic Meditation is presented in a clear, modern context and covers the work-a-day stuff frequently not addressed in other books. An essential text showing why incorporating meditation into contemporary life is something we need more than ever.'

Nathan Larson, film composer, author and musician

WHY
MEDITATE?

BECAUSE IT WORKS

JILLIAN LAVENDER

The information in this book is not intended to replace or conflict with the advice given to you by your GP or other health professional. All matters regarding your health should be discussed with your GP or other health professional. The author and publisher disclaim any liability directly or indirectly from the use of the material in this book by any person.

First published in Great Britain in 2021 by Yellow Kite
An Imprint of Hodder & Stoughton
An Hachette UK company

3

A CIP catalogue record for this title is available from the British Library

Hardback ISBN 978 1 529 35691 5
eBook ISBN 978 1 529 35692 2

Typeset in AVENIR by Manipal Technologies Limited

Printed and bound in Great Britain by Clays Ltd, Elcograf S.p.A.

Hodder & Stoughton policy is to use papers that are natural, renewable and recyclable products and made from wood grown in sustainable forests. The logging and manufacturing processes are expected to conform to the environmental regulations of the country of origin.

Yellow Kite
Hodder & Stoughton Ltd
Carmelite House
50 Victoria Embankment
London EC4Y 0DZ

www.yellowkitebooks.co.uk

TABLE OF CONTENTS

What this book is about

My name is Jillian Lavender and I'm a teacher of Vedic Meditation. Along with my partner Michael, I teach from my base in London and also regularly in New York. We have a daughter together and we're full-time teachers.

In my work, I meet people from all walks of life. The specific reasons why each person comes to learn to meditate are varied, yet there are some consistent themes. The underlying driver seems to be that people are searching for more in their lives – more happiness, clarity, energy, peace, health and success.

Sometimes they express this as wanting less – less stress, anxiety, pain, confusion, agitation. Ultimately they want to get rid of all that negativity so they can experience more positivity.

My message is simple. Meditation, when done properly, works. It isn't weird. Scientific evidence backs it up. Anyone can do it. It will positively change the way you feel and perform.

We hear a lot about meditation, yet there's still a lot of confusion about what it actually is. More than ever we're dealing with stress and overload. Everywhere you look you can see the effect of this build-up of tension. So many of the approaches to deal with these issues just aren't working.

We don't need more rules telling us how to behave. We don't need more talk. We need more action – tools that actually make a difference. We need knowledge that is relevant to our hectic lives and that enlivens our full potential. This is meditation – ancient knowledge for a modern world.

My story

Before we get started I'd like to share a bit about my journey up to this point. It's always helpful to know a little bit about the person who's doing the talking and there may be aspects of my experience that resonate for you.

I learned how to meditate in 1993 when I was living in Sydney, Australia.

Those who knew me then probably wouldn't have said I was an obvious candidate for meditation.

I didn't grow up with any spiritual education and I knew nothing about meditation. I didn't practise yoga, nor had I tried any alternative therapies. In fact, I was at the other end of the spectrum. Working long hours, going out a lot and, as an executive for a global publishing company, I spent my life on a plane. Really, I was a bit of a mess. Tired, stressed, overwhelmed, not very happy or healthy.

I heard about meditation through a friend's father. After years of battling insomnia he learned to meditate and within a few days he was sleeping. It was transforming his life. And everyone around him, including me, was noticing the changes.

So I went along to a talk at a nearby centre in Sydney. What I heard all made sense. I liked the straightforward, practical, scientifically validated nature of what I heard. There were no flowing robes or turbans and I could see the teachers were normal people. They were alert and yet calm at the same time. And I wanted some of that. So I jumped in and took the course.

I began to notice changes straight away. I'd always been a worrier, yet within a few weeks I could feel my anxiety levels dropping. I'd been feeling overwhelmed by my job and that began to shift. I was getting through my to-do list faster, tackling the jobs that were important, and letting go of stuff that didn't matter. Most of all I had more energy. I had been operating in a fog of jet lag and late nights and very little sleep. I hadn't realised how tired I was until I learned how to meditate. And I'd been stressed. But this was starting to change.

I continued meditating every day, and it became a part of my life. Just like brushing my teeth, I couldn't imagine not doing it. It was enjoyable and I looked forward to it. It continued to be an important tool as I was transferred to Paris, and then London.

After nearly a decade as a meditator in the corporate world, I decided to become a teacher. I had confirmed the benefits for myself and wanted to bring the knowledge and benefits to others. So I moved to a small cabin in Arizona, and spent fourteen months training closely with my teacher Thom Knoles, Maharishi Vyasanand Saraswati. In 2003 I moved back to London and began teaching. In 2008 the London Meditation Centre and the New York Meditation Center were opened, and these provide the base for my work worldwide.

This book will not teach you how to meditate

There's a lot of confusion and misunderstanding about what constitutes correct meditation. This book is about clearing up that confusion and inspiring you to take action to learn to meditate.

This book does NOT claim to teach you to meditate.

Unlike other books on meditation, this is a WHY DO not a how-to book.

There are plenty of books, apps and videos that claim to teach you to meditate. Some of my students started their meditation journey this way and got some initial value. But they were left searching for more. It's like the first rung on the ladder – it gets you going, but doesn't take you very far.

There is great value in getting things right from the beginning. Learning to meditate is one of the most fundamental and powerful tools we have to stay balanced and well. This is ancient knowledge, supported by modern science – wisdom of the ages that is more relevant than ever. You want to get it right. This is why I recommend learning from someone who is well trained and highly skilled. It's a subtle, delicate process and an important life skill. For this reason, how we go about learning deserves some care.

But why can't I learn to meditate from a book?

For the same reason you don't see people becoming expert piano players by reading books (or watching videos). You might be able to glean some pointers to get you going. You may pick up some of the language. But you're not going to become skilled and confident in your practice without the guidance of someone who knows how to teach correctly.

- Learning to meditate requires personal instruction. Although it's an effortless process, it's a delicate one, and it's not possible to communicate this adequately by written descriptions alone. The teacher needs to meet with the student in order to give guidance suited to the individual.
- Learning to meditate is experience-based. Everyone's experiences are unique, they learn at their own pace and the

teacher needs to support this so the student learns properly.

- It takes a while for the new meditator to be able to recognise and understand the experience of more subtle states of consciousness they're having. An experienced teacher is very important to guide and reassure so the meditator doesn't inadvertently undermine their progress.
- From the moment of initial instruction, experiences change and develop. It's crucial for the beginner student to be able to check in with a teacher who knows what they're doing.

This book is divided into three main parts.

Section 1: Meditation Myths
Before we dig into what meditation is, we need to clear up some common misconceptions. I call these Meditation Myths. A big part of understanding meditation is to understand what it is NOT.

Section 2: What is Meditation?
Here we get to the heart of what meditation is, and how it works. We'll look at this from three perspectives: mind, body and consciousness.

Section 3: Why Meditate?
I've highlighted 10 Reasons to Meditate, illustrating why meditation is the number-one tool to thrive in this hectic world.

Throughout the book I introduce you to meditators who share inspiring stories, demonstrating the potential of meditation. I've also included some powerful Starter Tips to get you going on your meditation journey. Finally, there's a Resources section so you can continue your research and find what works for you.

MEDITATION
MYTHS

I don't have time to meditate

When someone tells me this, I reply with a simple question: 'What's taking up all your time?'

The specific answers vary, and obvious things like work, children and general responsibilities of life come up. When we dig a bit deeper, we *always* find some wriggle room. There's time spent on stuff that's not so memorable, necessary or life-enhancing. (Read: social media!)

It comes down to the choices we're making about what's important, and the perceived payback on those investments. Time is your most precious resource. You have thirty minutes and then it's gone. You don't get that time back. How are you using it?

If you're so busy you don't have time to pause, rest and rebalance then something's off. Your life has 'unsustainable' written all over it!

Meditation doesn't have to involve many hours each day. Millions of people living very full lives are doing it. My meditation practice only takes about twenty minutes, twice a day. I typically do my first meditation early, before the day gets going. Then in the late afternoon/ early evening it's time for a second one. Meditating in the morning means I start the day clear, calm and energised. Then after a busy day, I wash away the stress and tiredness and enjoy my evening.

You might be reading this, thinking forty minutes a day! Where's that going to come from?

Don't panic. Meditators quickly notice that they gain time. The deep rest you get in a twenty-minute meditation leaves you more clear and alert. You get through your to-do list faster. You may even need to sleep less. Ultimately, you'll get more done. Investing in a few minutes of meditation delivers a return on productivity that's more than worth it.

Meditation means sitting in some weird position

When you look at pictures of people meditating you'll often see a yoga pose. Someone sitting with legs crossed, back perfectly straight, eyes closed, arms stretched out in front, hands contorted in some unusual gesture.

Actually none of this is necessary. You can practise meditation anywhere, sitting comfortably with the eyes closed. You might be in a chair at work, on the sofa at home or propped up in bed with pillows behind you.

This is wonderful because it means anyone can do it. You don't have to be some super-bendy yogi who has spent years perfecting how to sit in full lotus position.

It also means meditation is portable. You can take it on the move. You might be on a train on the way to work, on a plane, in a car (as long as you're not driving!) or on a park bench. Anywhere where you feel safe to sit down and close your eyes. You don't need to be in a soundproof room. You don't need to be in a yoga studio with crystals. The experience of millions of meditators all over the world shows this is something they can take with them anywhere, and integrate into their busy days.

meditation myth #3

It's not easy to meditate

Wrong!! This is the most common misunderstanding that I come across.

The idea that meditation is difficult and requires lots of discipline to control the mind is very common. And there are many techniques that do involve a focused approach like staring at an object, concentrating on the breath or trying to block out thoughts.

However, it doesn't have to be this way. Most importantly, there are huge benefits in NOT attempting to control, concentrate or focus the mind in meditation.

Meditation is a process of working *with* the nature of the mind instead of fighting against it. When we let the mind follow its natural instinct, it's possible for anyone to settle their mind spontaneously and effortlessly. All we need to take that inward dive is the proper technique. Then the process is easy and extremely pleasurable.

And here's the great thing: when something is easy and enjoyable you *want* to do it.

Many people come to us having tried meditation without success. In the vast majority of cases they've been doing something that involves effort. Their experiences are consistent: it wasn't easy, they didn't look forward to doing it, they were unsure if they were doing it correctly, and they didn't feel long-lasting, positive effects. It doesn't have to be this way.

This is such an important point. I'm going to come back to it in more detail later in the book. For now, let me say: **if you can think, you can meditate**.

Meditation is for New Age Hippies

All sorts of people meditate, from all walks of life: mothers, teachers, CEOs, nurses, actors, teenagers, you name it. All regular people, working, raising families, and being fully engaged in modern life.

It's understandable why many people think meditation is something just for hippies. Meditation exploded onto the scene in the 1960s. The Beatles learned to do it and there was a surge of young people who were drawn to it. It was the time of peace, love and happiness and meditation was accessible in a way that it had never been before. Millions were practising and starting to spread the word.

As time went on the importance of meditation became clear. A big reason this happened was the large body of scientific research that began to be published about the effects of meditation on health, brain functioning and emotional resilience. And of course, the world has become more hectic and demanding. There's an obvious need for everyone to have more peace and quiet in their lives.

There are no lifestyle requirements in order to be a meditator. You don't have to give up anything (or add anything) when you learn to meditate. It's not like we give you a rulebook and say, 'Okay, now you're a meditator, you have to stop drinking coffee and eat more kale.'

All you need to do is carve out a little time each day to sit and close the eyes. Then get on with your life with clarity and ease and make choices that feel right for you.

Meditation is a religion or a belief system

You don't need to believe in anything to meditate. It's not faith-based. I've taught people who identify with many different faiths and religions: Orthodox Jews, Buddhists, Christians, Catholics, Muslims and atheists.

The knowledge base from where we get meditation comes from India. But it's not Hindu, and it's not even an Indian philosophy. It doesn't mean you need to shave your head, change your name or use prayer beads.

In fact, you don't even have to believe meditation works for it to have an effect. All that's required is to do the practice. When you do, changes occur.

Now, it could be said that meditation is a spiritual practice. However it's important to have a clear definition of the word spiritual. I don't mean dogma or a religious institution or a belief system. I mean your spirit, your essence.

For many people life is mainly experienced at the level of the mind and body, with little awareness of something deeper and more subtle. Meditation is a technique that allows you to access a deeper aspect of yourself that underpins your mind and body – your least excited state of consciousness.

At your essence you are conscious. To be conscious means to be. It is the fundamental level of your existence and the source of everything. Meditation puts you in touch with this place, your essence. In this light, it is a profoundly spiritual practice.

It takes ages to see results

Often people believe that for something to be really worthwhile it must take a lot of time and effort. The idea is that if it's good, it's going to be difficult.

Here's an email I got from a potential student, talking about this concern:

> I've attended yoga trainings and meditation retreats in the hope that by doing so, I will find some peace in my head. I practised for a while and then stopped, started and then stopped again. Maybe it's because anything that's good takes a long time, lots of effort and discipline in order to see change.

A regular meditation practice does involve a willingness to make the time each day. However, meditation isn't something you need to do for months and months before you start to get it and notice a shift. With the right training and technique, even in the early days you'll notice the positive effects. The benefits of experiencing inner quiet and calm arrive swiftly.

In teaching thousands of people to meditate, I see this time and again. In the first few days of learning to meditate, students report changes.

Meditators find it quickly becomes a regular part of their day. Just like having a shower each morning, you find yourself wanting to do it. It feels good when you do it, others are happy you've done it and you feel better for the rest of the day.

Here's a comment from a student after *one* week of meditation:

> I felt a surge of energy this week that I honestly have not experienced for months… I also feel more focused, patient, and less irritable. Above all, I feel hopeful and happy with less anxiety.

Running is my meditation

No, it's not.

What's happening in your body when you meditate is very different to what's happening when you run (or lift weights, or swim, or cycle, or do any other exercise). Meditation is about de-excitation. Exercise is about excitation.

From an evolutionary perspective, human beings ran as part of the survival mechanism. The only time you needed to move fast was to chase food or get away from predators. Running as a sport or exercise is a relatively recent development.

I understand why running feels good and why someone might think of it as a way of tuning out. When you're in fight-or-flight mode you're not speculating about the future or replaying the past. When your ancestor was running away from a bear they weren't thinking about tomorrow or worrying about yesterday. Their body was having an automatic stress reaction that brought them to the present moment. When you go for a run, a part of you believes you're running away from something. So you stop thinking about the mortgage or ruminating about what someone said in yesterday's meeting.

When you run, your metabolic rate increases. Heart rate goes up. Blood pressure rises. The prefrontal cortex in your brain shuts down. You stop worrying about the mortgage. You stop rehashing the past. Endorphins course through the bloodstream to compensate for the stress the body is under. It feels good; however, the purpose is to mask an underlying experience of stress.

The *opposite* happens when you meditate. The science is very clear. The body rests deeply and the front part of the brain lights up in a powerful way. The biochemistry of the body is the opposite of stress. Rather than fight-or-flight it is one of rest-and-digest.

WHAT IS MEDITATION?

Now that we've unpicked the most common misunderstandings about meditation, we're beginning to get a sense of what meditation is:

- Natural
- Easy
- Available to anyone
- Deeply restful and nourishing
- Backed up by scientific research
- And not weird!

Now it's time to dive deeper and find out what meditation is all about.

Not all meditations are the same

I've been teaching meditation since 2003. In that time I've seen an explosion in the number of techniques and practices labelled as meditation. It's not hard to see why. There's an urgent need to counterbalance the rollercoaster of life in a way that actually works and doesn't have negative side-effects.

Much of the growth in meditation is in mindfulness-based approaches, now a multibillion-dollar industry. Originating in the Buddhist tradition, mindfulness has been packaged in a way that makes it more secular and accessible.

The other stand-out area of expansion is the 'meditation app' approach. The market for these apps is huge and it's an easy way to access mindfulness or guided techniques.

On balance I think it's positive that there's more awareness about meditation. The watch-out is that with so much demand, the market fills up with products of varying quality and effectiveness. I see many things that are called meditation that have little positive impact. Many techniques don't deliver because the fundamentals aren't in place. This results in confusion and misunderstanding about the value of all meditations. It might also mean someone tries something and when it doesn't work they think meditation is not for them, when the fault actually lies in having had a suboptimal experience.

Three approaches to meditation

Broadly there are three main styles of meditation:

i. Concentration or Focused Attention
    It's in the name. This approach involves fixing your attention on something with the aim of not thinking about anything else. It might be concentrating on a candle, staring at an image or simply focusing on your breath. The goal is to create and maintain a state of silence. This approach takes effort and discipline to maintain. In my experience, people often find it too hard and abandon the process pretty quickly.
ii. Open Monitoring
    This approach is also known as mindfulness. Open monitoring meditation directs the meditator's awareness to feelings, thoughts or breathing, with a mood of non-judgement and detachment. The practitioner looks to maintain a sense of calm in the midst of a thought-filled mind. The goal is to become more grounded by developing awareness of the present moment, rather than overreacting to the situation.
iii. Automatic Self-Transcending
    This is the meditation style I practise and teach. It involves the use of a sound called a mantra to orient the mind towards

quieter levels of thinking. The mantra is like a vehicle that the mind hops onto, and automatically the mind moves with the mantra to experience finer and finer layers of thinking. A point comes when the mantra disappears and the mind falls quiet. This is a state of pure inner contentedness for the mind. The mind is alert however there are no thoughts going on.

Different meditations have different effects

Just as different meditation techniques are approached and practised differently, they also produce very different effects on the mind and body.

When I examine different techniques, there are three aspects I look at:

1. What's the effect on brain functioning?
   The brain is the most important organ in the human body, governing and coordinating our thoughts and actions at the centre of the nervous system. Therefore it makes sense to know what impact a particular practice is having on the brain. Through the use of neural imaging and EEG we can see different parts of the brain are activated and developed with each of these styles.
2. How deeply are you resting?
   For me one of the most important benefits of meditation is the deep rest that I get, much deeper than sleep. I know how much better I feel and perform when I'm well rested, so having a regular way of resting deeply is key.
3. Is it easy, enjoyable and practical?
   Perhaps this is the most important of all. Meditation only works when you do it. Is it easy? Do you look forward to meditating? Or does it feel like hard work? Can you fit this in to your life?

When I lecture, I'll often ask: 'How many people have tried meditation?' About eight out of ten hands go up. Then I ask: 'And how many of you are meditating every day?' Maybe one hand stays up. Yes, meditation is popular, but finding a practice that you are motivated to do and that fits with your lifestyle can be challenging.

I know if meditation wasn't easy and enjoyable I wouldn't give it the priority I do. I look forward to meditating every day because it feels good to do it. Even more important, I feel better having done it.

In this book I'm going to be focusing on the category of automatic self-transcending meditation.

In my experience this style of meditation ticks all of these boxes. As we'll see later in the book:

√ brain functioning is optimised
√ it delivers a profound level of rest, deeper than sleep
√ it's easy, enjoyable and fits with a busy life

Where does meditation come from?

To understand this we must go back at least 5,000 years. In a region near the Indus Valley (what is known today as India and Pakistan), there were large, well-organised groups of people. This civilisation was organised into hierarchical systems around food supply, crafts, trades and art and culture. Behind all this there was a knowledge base that supported the development of the citizens in all aspects of their life including spirituality, health, architecture and music. Techniques such as meditation and yoga were a fundamental part of daily life. This body of knowledge was referred to as the Veda.

In the ancient language of Sanskrit, Veda means 'pure knowledge'. It is the oldest continuous tradition of knowledge in human history, pre-dating Western civilisation and scientific knowledge by thousands of years.

While there are written records of the Vedic knowledge, called the Vedas, the essence of the knowledge has been passed on in an oral tradition from generation to generation. Unlike Western scientific discovery, which uses formal processes of observation, experimentation and measurement, the Veda was directly cognised by enlightened men and women. Their laboratory was their own mind and body and their research involved going deep into their own awareness. Their tools of experimentation were techniques of consciousness, meditation being the most powerful.

What these ancient seers discovered was the essence of life itself. They had the refined apparatus of such pure minds and bodies that they were able to experience the subtlest layers of creation. By settling down to the deepest levels of their minds they were able perceive how the fundamental laws of nature operate. This knowledge is the Veda – knowledge of how the laws of nature function at every layer of creation. When we understand the patterns of nature that are at work in our world, we're able to align ourselves with them and enjoy a more frictionless flow. We enjoy the support of nature rather than struggling against life. An essential tool for becoming more acquainted with these laws of nature is meditation.

a word about:

Yoga

In India, yoga is recognised as part of the vast body of Vedic knowledge. However, in the West it has generally been reduced to only one aspect, hatha yoga, the physical postures. These poses are called 'asanas' and when you practise them regularly, they build strength, balance and flexibility in the whole body. Specific breathing techniques are also employed along with the poses to settle the nervous system and integrate the mind and body.

However, to view yoga as merely a physical practice barely scratches the surface of what it's all about. The literal translation of the word yoga is 'union'. To unify means to bring together, to amalgamate, to join, to fuse. The question arises: what is being unified with what?

According to the knowledge of yoga, our true nature lies beyond the limited boundaries of the material, everyday experience of life. There's more to us than what we can see on the surface. Yoga says the truth lies deep within – a vast reservoir of pure, serene, inner bliss. Pure consciousness – the source of all life. Yoga calls it 'the Self' (with a capital S).

Yoga is the means of unifying our individual personality (small self) with this universal unbounded big Self within. And meditation is the most important technique to bring about this merger. The yoga postures were a way to prepare the body for meditation and allow the mind to take a deeper dive.

So what does meditation look like?

Early this morning I meditated before our daughter woke up and prior to breakfast.

Here's what happened:

I sat on the sofa with a cushion behind me so my back was supported. I sat comfortably and my head and shoulders were upright. I had a little clock next to me so I could take a peek to track the time. I closed my eyes and took a few seconds to settle. Then I began to think my mantra silently (no chanting or speaking it aloud).

I felt my breathing slow down, my body relax. Various thoughts popped into my mind. I was aware of noises, but they didn't bother me. I checked the clock a couple of times to see how many minutes had gone past and after twenty minutes it was time to end the meditation. I let go of thinking my mantra and kept my eyes closed for a few minutes. I then slowly opened my eyes and I was done. Ready for the day.

If anyone had walked in on me while I was meditating they would have seen someone sitting quietly with her eyes closed. Nothing that looked exotic or unusual. This is a big part of why you can do this anywhere. Many of our students will meditate on their commute – trains and planes are great places to meditate!

Meditation and The Mind

How does it work?

In this style of meditation we don't do much.

We sit down, close the eyes and think the mantra. The mind very quickly begins to settle down. As a result, the body moves to a relaxed state. This process is automatic and effortless. The thought that leads us on that inward journey is a simple, mean-ingless sound – a mantra.

The mantra is the key

Mantra is a Sanskrit word that means an 'instrument for the mind'. *'Man'* comes from the Sanskrit word for mind and *'tra'* means vehi-cle or instrument. It's where we get our English words 'traction' and 'tractor'. The mantra has traction or pulling power for the mind.

A mantra is a sound that produces a known effect

There are many different types of mantras, used in different ways, with different outcomes. There are mantras designed to be spoken out loud that have a particular effect on the mind, body and environment. Other mantras involve imagining a cer-tain goal such as peace, love and happiness in order to enliven those qualities. Some mantras are even designed to purify the air and bestow blessings on our food and surroundings.

In the automatic self-transcending style of meditation, we use a particular type of mantra designed to settle the mind. The mantra is a simple, meaningless sound that's chosen for each meditator by their teacher. It is a particular pulsation of sound that resonates with the thinker. Certain sounds work best for certain groups of people.

You close the eyes and silently begin to think the sound. Imme-diately and spontaneously, it begins to self-refine and quieten down. As you gently repeat it, the sound becomes more soft and subtle until a point is reached where it's almost impercep-tible. And then it does its last little trick, and it disappears, and for a moment the mind falls quiet. The mind drops into an inner, serene state where you're conscious and awake and yet you're not thinking. Those moments don't tend to last so long and often you're not even aware it's happening.

I refer to the mantra very specifically as a sound (not a word) because it has no meaning – it's a pure sound. There's no literal or connotative meaning that the mind can latch on to. If the mantra held meaning for the meditator it would keep the mind active and engaged, thinking about the meaning, rather than leading the mind away from thinking to increasingly more subtle layers of cognition.

How does the mantra lead the mind inward?

The process of meditating involves turning the attention away from the outer world towards the inner, more subtle layers of the mind. The mantra is the device that orients the mind on this inward dive.

The primary quality of the mantra is the tendency to become quieter. This self-refining capability is built into the structure of the sound itself. When you think it silently in the mind, it spontaneously becomes fainter.

In addition to this, the mantra has another very important quality that's key to how it works. As it becomes more subtle and soft, it becomes increasingly fascinating and soothing to the mind. The phenomenology of experiencing the mantra causes it to become more charming.

The charm of the vertical dive

Because of the personal nature of the sound, the mantra is *attractive* to the mind. As it becomes increasingly quiet it becomes more and more charming. Eventually a point is reached where the mantra is absolutely fascinating to the mind and yet at the same time so faint, it's almost imperceptible. And then it disappears and the mind is left with no mantra and no thought replacing it.

To fully understand how this works we need to take a step back and understand the nature of the mind.

This is important for a number of reasons:

- When we know how the mind works we can align with it, rather than fighting against it.
- By understanding what the mind wants, we can deliver exactly what the mind desires.
- When we're in sync with the true nature of the mind we don't waste precious time and energy doing something that's only going to be a struggle.

In this meditation we work with the mind rather than fighting against it.

What is the mind looking for?

Quite simply, your mind is looking for happiness. This is why you think.

The mind doesn't move randomly – it has purpose. The basis of all thinking is the natural desire of the mind to move in the direction of greater wholeness. When there's a choice, the attention always moves towards that which is more fascinating.

Any time you're conscious, your mind will be able to detect perceived greater happiness and it will move in that direction (whether the source of happiness is sustainable or not).

Imagine while you're sitting reading this book, someone starts to play your favourite song in the next room. Spontaneously your mind will move towards the source of charm – the beautiful melody. As fascinating as this book is, your mind detects greater happiness and goes there, effortlessly.

But what about those times when you find yourself thinking about a problem, something not happy? If the mind is looking for happiness, why do we sometimes find ourselves caught up in thinking about things that we'd rather not think about, like bills that need to be paid or some rude comment that someone made?

When you're thinking about a problem, it's in search of a solution to that problem. The reason you find yourself thinking about the issue is because of the conviction that if you ruminate on it one more time you'll work out a solution. And in finding the solution, the 'problem' will go away and you'll experience bliss.

The mind persistently engages in thinking that allows it to move to greater happiness. And if more happiness can be gained through yet another step, we'll think yet another thought.

How do you use the mantra?

There are many styles of meditation that use a mantra, so it's important to explore how we use the mantra in this type of automatic self-transcending meditation.

How you use the mantra is as important as what it is

The majority of mantra-based practices involve the constant repetition of a sound. In Sanskrit this is referred to as 'japa' meditation. The mantra may be chanted or repeated very softly or silently, in a continuous repetitive flow. Very often the practitioner uses a string of beads as a tool to support the constant rhythm of the mind and keep track of the number of repetitions. This kind of practice tends to keep the mind engaged at more active, surface layers of thinking.

In the style of meditation that I teach, we do not practise japa. Rather than striving to constantly focus the mind on a sound or idea, the mantra, used effortlessly, allows the attention to settle down.

The mantra is an orienting device, not a concentration device

It leads the mind in the direction of a supremely restful and refined state, instead of holding the mind in an active and focused mode.

Controlling the mind is hard work

You may have heard people talk about the concept of the 'monkey mind'. This is the idea that the mind behaves like a naughty monkey – out of control, constantly moving, jumping from branch to branch. This is supposedly why we find ourselves caught up in thinking all the time: like the monkey, the mind is unable to keep still, concentrate and experience calm.

And yet have you ever tried to catch a wandering monkey? It's a mistake to think that racing around, waving a stick and trying to force it into a cage is going to work. Much better to entice it with some delicious bananas; it will come to you of its own accord, easily and with no effort on your part.

It's the same for your mind. To assume the mind is mischievous and out of control leads to all sorts of techniques to try to tame it into being quiet. In order to 'tie it down' a great deal of effort is required. As a result, various practices aimed at controlling the mind have developed over time. And these techniques are hard work.

Many of these fall into the category of focused attention techniques. Common examples are to concentrate on the breath or focus on a particular image. Those who have tried these approaches report it's difficult to stay focused. It takes a lot of effort and they may give up out of frustration and tiredness. Often people say they feel more wound up than when they started!

We can see how this works by performing a very simple exercise:

Close the eyes and notice your breath. Then, stop thinking. Just for a moment, stop the thoughts in your mind. Take a moment and try it right now.

Within a few seconds you feel how useless this is. A paradox immediately presents itself. If the aim is to stop the thoughts, then 'I mustn't think' is a thought, and you end up in a circular loop of thinking-about-not-thinking. The effect ends up being the opposite of what you intended. By continually trying to push something away, you end up highlighting the very thing you don't want. The mind, by its nature, will find something to think about. Your mind cannot be active without content.

So what if we offer the mind something fascinating?

Give the mind something charming to follow

What makes an automatic self-transcending style of meditation different to these concentration-based techniques is that we offer the mind something inherently attractive. Those inner, quiet layers of thinking are delicious for the mind. So rather than straining and trying to force the mind to be quiet, the mantra leads the mind towards the inner layers of subtlety and peace by giving it a vehicle to move in that direction, naturally and spontaneously.

Work with the nature of the mind rather than against it

No effort or control is required. As we've seen in the exercise above, control and force simply leave the mind active and frustrated because it's impossible to force the mind inwards. Using effort only increases mental activity, which keeps the mind up at the surface and inhibits the process of allowing the mind to settle down.

First bliss, then the thoughts will stop

The desire for a peaceful mind is natural. We live in an increasingly frenetic world and it's common to feel overrun by the constant chitter-chatter in the mind. When you can't switch off the mental noise it leaves you unable to focus and prioritise. Many people end up in a state of nervous exhaustion.

Maybe you've had the thought: 'If only I could stop all the thoughts then I'd have some peace. I just wish I could switch my brain off!'

As we've just seen, trying not to think doesn't work. 'Don't think' is a thought that leaves you in a more agitated state.

So how do you stop the thoughts?

The answer is all to do with sequence. Like anything in life, sequence is very important. If two people have all the right ingredients to make a cake and yet only one of them knows the correct order in which to arrange and mix those ingredients, there's only going to be one cake worth eating!

In meditation, there's also an important sequence that holds the key to unlocking the full potential of the mind.

Let's revisit two important points:

• your mind is constantly on the move, seeking something more fascinating
• trying not to think is hard work and ultimately futile

So where does this leave us?

Rather than trying to force thoughts to stop, we need to understand the mind and work with it. The sequential flow of the mind works like this:

Stage 1:
The mind engages in thinking in order to find more happiness. By introducing something fascinating to the mind (the mantra), the mind naturally moves in that direction.

Stage 2:
As the mantra refines, the mind begins to enjoy greater levels of happiness. A point is reached when the mind is so saturated in bliss, it's unable to conceive of anything more charming.

Stage 3:
Then the thoughts stop. The mind is still conscious and capable of having a thought. However, no thoughts come because the mind has achieved its goal.

So this turns everything upside down. Rather than trying to get rid of those pesky thoughts in aid of a bit of peace, it's actually the opposite.

First the mind experiences bliss. Then, *as a result* of this experience, the thoughts stop. Consciousness without thought must be bliss, because if it wasn't, thoughts would occur.

Silence is a product of bliss

Your mind becomes more quiet as it experiences more and more bliss. By orienting the mind towards progressively greater happiness, the mind reaches a point in which it is satiated. In this state, the mind is unable to conceive of anything more blissful. All thoughts stop. Activity stops. A state of least-excitation is experienced.

Why use sound to settle the mind?

The five senses – hearing, sight, taste, touch and smell – act as a gateway to experience the world. They each allow a range of sensory experiences, from the very explicit all the way to extremely subtle levels.

In ancient Vedic texts known as the Upanishads, sound is recommended as the means of bringing the mind to more settled states. One reason for this is that the senses are hierarchically ordered in terms of subtlety, and hearing is the most refined. It's the first sense we experience as a foetus; parents instinctively sing to the belly of a pregnant woman. It's also the last to fall away when the body dies; in many spiritual traditions people pray or read sacred texts to the dying, knowing the words can be heard.

In meditation we have an intention to think a very particular sound. This mantra is a thought of a sound that has been internalised. And because hearing is the subtlest of the senses, it's the most effective way to lead the mind to less excited states of consciousness. In its most subtle state, the mantra is extremely compelling and this is what draws the mind to this quietest point.

Meditation and The Body

As is the mind, so is the body

We know that the immune system, like the central nervous system, has memory and the capacity to learn. Thus, it could be said that intelligence is located not only in the brain but in cells that are distributed throughout the body, and that the traditional separation of mental processes from the body, including emotions, is no longer valid.

Candace Pert, *Molecules of Emotion*

While many scientists and medical professionals now acknowledge the connection between mind and body, it's taking time for this to be reflected in the mainstream. It's not so long ago that physics and philosophy considered the mind and body to be completely separate. What someone was thinking had nothing to with their body, and what was going on in the body was in no way related to the workings of the mind. We now know that mind and body are highly interdependent.

For every state of the mind there is a corresponding state in the body

Imagine a mind that's full of agitation and anxiety, worrying about something. Instantaneously, molecules are released and these chemical messengers go out to the cells of the body, delivering a message of fear. The cells of the body spontaneously respond by printing out that neurochemistry of fear. Within seconds the fearful mind has created a fearful body.

As Candace Pert describes in her book *Molecules of Emotion*, 'A feeling sparked in your mind will translate as a peptide being released somewhere. Peptides regulate every aspect of your body, from whether you're going to digest your food properly to whether you're going to destroy a tumor cell.'

Every mental and emotional event initiates a cascade of these chemicals, flooding the system with information about how to respond. Angry, sad and fearful thoughts and feelings are particularly draining and damaging for the body. Happy, relaxed and kind thoughts and feelings are nourishing and life-enhancing.

You are what you think
The mind and body are like parallel universes – anything that happens in the mental universe will leave tracks in the physical one.

An agitated mind leads to an agitated body. An angry mind leads to an angry body. The body is very quickly a reflection of what's happening in the more subtle realm of thinking. Every time you think, you're initiating a pattern of reactions within the body. Your body is the physical picture in 3D of what you've been thinking.

And the opposite is also true. What's happening in your body will affect how you think.

For every state of the body there is a corresponding state in the mind

Think of how you feel when you come down with a full-on head cold. Your sinuses are blocked, you're sneezing and your body feels achey and feverish. How easy is it to focus your mind? How patient and loving are you? How productive are you, as you try to get through your work? As your body struggles to fight off the bugs, your mental functioning is compromised, leaving you feeling unmotivated and unable to concentrate. After a few days, the cold has gone and you feel mentally alert and you're less likely to be overwhelmed by the demands of your day. Your mind is sharper and clearer based on your body being well.

When the mind settles down, the body rests

As we've seen, meditation is a practice that begins with turning down the volume of the mind. The mantra leads the mind on an inward dive, away from the busy, conscious layers of thinking towards an increasingly quiet mind. Thinking becomes fainter and softer. More quiet thinking has a direct effect on the body.

As the mind settles, the body begins to rest

Within a few minutes, the meditator's physiology is resting much deeper than sleep. For me, this was one of the biggest benefits when I first learned to meditate. Prior to meditation I was constantly tired, so the energy I gained was a game changer.

Here's a comment from a student who describes the effect of meditation on her energy levels after *one* week of meditation:

> After the first week the effects were so profound that nothing was going to stop me meditating. It was really simple – I had so much more energy there was no way I wasn't going to do it. It gives me such a boost in the afternoon, making me much more efficient with my time, that it's totally worth carving out that twenty minutes to meditate.

Deeper rest than sleep

One of the most accurate ways to understand how deeply someone is resting is to measure their oxygen metabolism. This is the rate at which the body consumes energy. If you're more active, your metabolic rate will be higher. If you're resting it will be lower. The primary fuel in the body is oxygen and this is why the standard means of determining your metabolic rate is to look at the levels of oxygen consumption. If you start running down the road, your demand for fuel to fund that activity goes up and you consume more oxygen. Therefore your metabolic rate increases. When you meditate you move into a very restful state, and oxygen metabolism decreases.

It was previously understood that there is a minimum level at which the metabolism can operate – referred to as the basal metabolic rate. Think of it as the absolute bare minimum of energy that's needed to keep you going when you're sitting still. When you sleep, the basal metabolic rate drops by about 8 to 10 per cent and this was thought to be about the lowest level at which we can sustain ourselves.

This is why the editor of the medical journal *The Lancet* initially rejected the findings of the first ever study on an automatic self-transcending technique, by Dr John Allison in 1969. Dr Allison measured the drop in oxygen consumption to be twice as much as that which occurs in normal sleep. This drop in the amplitude of breath was regarded as so abnormal that the editor pointed out to him in a letter that his figures for oxygen consumption were 'incompatible with life'! However, Dr Allison's findings were eventually validated and published in *The Lancet* as a letter in 1970.

Subsequent studies backed up this pioneering research demonstrating that the metabolic rate drops quickly – within about five minutes of beginning to meditate. What's most fascinating is that the drop in oxygen consumption is greater than what someone would experience after sleeping for six hours. A few minutes of meditation, and the meditator is resting at a level deeper than what would have taken hours to achieve from regular sleep. This is VERY deep rest, gained very efficiently.

I love this description from our student Wac, about the energising effect of meditation:

Meditation empowers me. It's like one of those electric cars you see plugged into a socket getting charged. I feel I have plugged into Mother Earth, recharging my batteries so I can then help everyone around me.

Slowing down of heart rate

Another obvious way to look at how rested the body is is to look at what happens to heart rate. Not surprisingly, as the metabolic rate drops, the heart rate decreases – some studies show an average drop of five beats per minute. This is the opposite of what happens when you're in the hyper-excited state of a stress reaction, where heart rate increases.

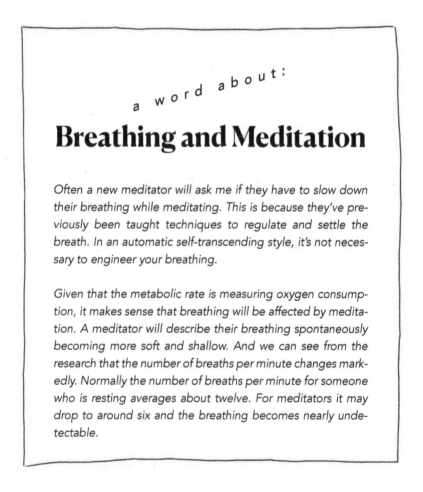

a word about:

Breathing and Meditation

Often a new meditator will ask me if they have to slow down their breathing while meditating. This is because they've previously been taught techniques to regulate and settle the breath. In an automatic self-transcending style, it's not necessary to engineer your breathing.

Given that the metabolic rate is measuring oxygen consumption, it makes sense that breathing will be affected by meditation. A meditator will describe their breathing spontaneously becoming more soft and shallow. And we can see from the research that the number of breaths per minute changes markedly. Normally the number of breaths per minute for someone who is resting averages about twelve. For meditators it may drop to around six and the breathing becomes nearly undetectable.

The important point here is that when meditating you don't need to do anything to change your breathing. It will automatically slow down, as a consequence of how deeply rested you are.

There are other powerful practices that start with the breath as a way to calm the mind and body. My good friend and student, Sophie Dear, is a wonderful yoga teacher and she has kindly shared a very simple and effective breathing technique to help ground you in the midst of very demanding moments.

starter tip

The 4:6 Breath

You can do this from wherever you are – at work, at home, on the train. This is a lovely soothing breath that brings a sense of calm and peace. It's great to do when you're feeling a little bit stressed or anxious.

Find somewhere where you can sit or lie down comfortably and close the eyes.

Take a moment to acquaint yourself with your breath as it is now. Is your breathing shallow, smooth, stop-start? Simply take notice, without judgement.

Now gently start the practice of breathing in for a slow count of four, and exhaling for a slow count of six. Repeat this cycle, feeling an expansion in the body on the inhale, and a release on the exhale. Notice how your body feels as you do this. If your mind's wandering all over the place, this is totally normal. Gently come back to your breath and the body when this happens. You can spend anywhere between three and five minutes practising this pattern of breathing.

We tend to spend most of our day operating from our sympathetic nervous system – the 'fight-or-flight' mode. By bringing a longer exhale to our breathing, we're stimulating our parasympathetic nervous system – our 'rest-and-digest' mode. We can use the breath to very quickly change the state of our nervous system, and restore a little bit of balance to our life.

When the body rests, the body purifies and normalises

Everything you do is affected by how well rested you are. Rest is the basis of all your activity. This delicate balance between rest and activity is essential for the nervous system to stay healthy and in optimal working order. Activity is the means for us to express ourselves and find meaning and fulfilment in life. Rest is the means by which we restore energy and recover from the effects of the day.

Rest is often thought of as not doing anything. I don't agree. Knowing how to rest deeply and efficiently is one of the greatest skills you can gain because rest is the funding mechanism that supports you in everything you do. Without good-quality rest, your performance and well-being will be undermined.

Regular sleep is no longer enough to clear out the negative effects of daily stress and strain. Our lives are so demanding and we're experiencing a huge load each day. No wonder stress and exhaustion accumulate in the system. Sleep is just not enough to clear out the deeper-rooted stress and fatigue. This is where meditation makes the difference.

Recovery from overload

When you rest, your system knows what to do. The body automatically normalises itself whenever it has the opportunity. And it will do so to the maximum possible extent – it all depends on how much rest it gets.

Let's say I have a foam ball in my hand and I squeeze it. In physics we call this applying a load. By squeezing the ball, the shape is distorted and its structure changes. This change in structure is said to create an increase in potential energy. When I release my hand and 'relax' the ball, this energy is released and the structure resumes its original shape. This same scientific principle applies to our bodies when they're subjected to overload or pressure.

When your body is subjected to excitation and overload it accumulates stress, and this produces a physical change or distortion in your system. Just like with the foam ball, when you 'relax' the body and allow stress to dissolve, the energy that was stored in the stress is released, resulting in a temporary increase in activity in the body.

A meditator will experience this release in a number of different ways depending on the stress that's being released. Very often it won't even be noticed because it's so subtle. However, sometimes the increase in activity will be felt as a sensation in the physiology. It's fascinating how often students will notice sensations in their neck, shoulders and back in their very first meditation. These are such common places where we store stress, as we hunch over a laptop or carry a heavy load, that they end up being stress hotspots in the body.

Other times the activity of stress dissolution will be experienced as corresponding activity in the brain and the meditator notes this as a thought in meditation. It could be about anything – a random thought or a mental image that suddenly pops into the mind. This is why we don't fight against thoughts in this technique. We don't try to push them away because they're an indicator that something very valuable is happening – the body is releasing stress.

I often refer to the process of de-excitation that happens in the mind and body via meditation as like turning down the 'temperature' on the mind and body. This is where physics again helps us to understand what's happening when we rest so deeply.

The Third Law of Thermodynamics is a general principle of purification that shows that as temperature is reduced, purity and order increase. When you reduce the temperature in a structure, disorderliness is removed. All materials may be purified of any irregularities by taking them to their state of least excitation, which is a state of perfect order or zero entropy.

The profoundly deep rest of meditation aligns with this concept of spontaneous purification. Turn down the 'temperature' of the body and any irregularities in the form of stresses are quickly unmasked and removed.

a word about:

Maintaining Balance

It's possible to get too much of a good thing. We all know that drinking water is good for us. Drink a couple of litres a day and you'll be doing yourself a service. Drink twenty litres and you'll be harming yourself. Regular exercise is important for your health and longevity. Overdoing it and exercising too much will actually have the opposite effect, causing the body to wear out more quickly.

As always in life, balance is key.

Equally, we don't want to meditate too much. The 'recommended dose' is twice a day for about twenty minutes each time. If you do more you'll upset the balance between rest and activity. Rather than becoming more engaged and effective, you'll actually become less available for life and less able to function at a high level.

Meditation and Consciousness

Where do thoughts come from?

A thought starts from the deepest level of consciousness and rises through the whole depth of the ocean of mind until it finally appears as a conscious thought at the surface.

Maharishi Mahesh Yogi

We all have many thoughts every day. We don't know exactly how many, but estimates range from 50,000 to 80,000 thoughts – per person, every day!

What is a thought?

A thought has two aspects. Every thought is both a stream of *energy* and an expression of *intelligence*. We know thoughts have energy because there's a process involved. Wherever there's a process, there is a consumption of energy. A process starts with more energy at the beginning and has less energy at the end. We measure energy in a thought by using an electro-encephalogram (EEG) to track electrical activity in the brain. To put it simply, thinking takes energy.

However, a thought is not just an indiscriminate explosion of energy. A thought comprises intelligence, because every cognition has a discriminating value. It's about something particular, it has meaning. A thought is energy that is directed to something specific.

So where do all these thoughts come from?

Without consciousness there is no thinking. It's not possible to have a thought when you're unconscious. You can stimulate a cadaver as much as you like, but there's no thinking going on. Likewise, if someone is in a coma they don't think.

Therefore you must be conscious in order to think.

Think of your mind as an ocean. The surface layers of the ocean are active, churned up and covered in waves. As you dive deep down you experience progressively quieter layers of activity until you reach the silent, peaceful sea floor. Like the ocean, the mind is also more active at the surface, conscious level. The deeper, inner levels of the mind become progressively more quiet and refined until a baseline of silence is reached.

A thought is an excitation of consciousness. The process of thinking starts from the deepest level of consciousness as a faint impulse, and becomes more explicit as it moves towards the surface of the mind. As it rises up, it gains more and more structure and meaning until it appears on the surface, conscious level, where it's appreciated as a distinct cognition.

Consciousness is the source of your thoughts

Normally you're only aware of your thoughts in their fully developed form when they've reached the surface of the mind. However, those thoughts must logically have gone through prior stages of development. Meditation involves orienting the mind towards those earlier, subtler stages. The thousands of thoughts you have each day come from the deepest aspect of your mind. This pure state of consciousness is the source of all your thoughts – a transcendental state that lies beyond thinking. A state of Being.

a word about:

Source vs Cause of Thought

There is a distinction between the source of thought and the cause of the thought. As I've explained, every thought begins from the deepest levels of the mind. Those tens of thousands of thoughts you're having every day start as faint impulses in the mind and become more discrete and structured until they burst into the gross conscious levels of the mind.

However, source and cause are not the same.

The trigger for your thoughts is your environment. I see that person crossing the street and I have a thought: 'Oh look, there's Joe.' The thought didn't come from over there. Although the environment may stimulate your thoughts, the environment is not the thinker. The environment provides the stimuli that leads you to have a thought. Consciousness is the source of the thought itself.

As you move closer to a source of light like a lamp, the light becomes stronger. In the same way, as you move towards the source of thought, the thoughts become stronger. By catching those subtle impulses of thought in earlier stages you're able to access more subtlety and refinement. Thinking becomes richer and this translates into more powerful and effective action.

When you experience that pure state which is the source of creative intelligence in the mind, you are experiencing the home of your own creativity. The fountainhead of your own discriminating and differentiating ability. You're experiencing the source of mental energy in your own mind rather than the product, the thoughts.

What lies beyond the mind?

When the mind has settled, we are established in our essential nature, which is unbounded consciousness. Our essential nature is usually overshadowed by the activity of the mind.

The Yoga Sutras of Patanjali, translated by Alistair Shearer

Though consciousness is self-evident – you know you're conscious – it's a concept that's often hard to grasp. The mind is usually so full of thoughts that we never get the chance to experience the least-excited condition of consciousness – a silent, pure state, undiluted by thoughts.

It's like when you go to the cinema. There's a white screen up there with a movie playing on it. The movie is so fascinating you don't notice the screen in the background, even though you know it's there. You don't see the screen because the images of the movie overshadow it. However, if you shone a very bright light on the middle of the screen, it would reveal the white screen behind the play of images.

Consciousness is like the screen on which the imagery of thinking plays out. Thinking itself is not the screen; thinking is the activity that obscures the backdrop of your essential nature – pure consciousness.

Consciousness is a quantity and we want more of it

Rather than a limited binary view of consciousness (conscious or unconscious), there are infinite grades of consciousness. The degree to which we're conscious affects every aspect of life. Naturally we want to be more conscious rather than less conscious.

Let's take an exaggerated example to prove the point. Say someone has been drinking vodka tonics all afternoon. In an inebriated state, awareness has narrowed down and he has a much reduced capacity to think clearly, let alone creatively. If we keep narrowing down his consciousness by injecting him with tranquillisers we can get to a state of unconsciousness. Now there is zero ability to conceptualise. The degree of consciousness is directly related to the ability to think clearly.

The quality of your thinking depends upon the quantity of your consciousness

More clear, less diluted consciousness creates thoughts that are strong and intelligent. If our awareness is limited and obstructed, then the thoughts that come forth will be weak and unbalanced. Stress and fatigue create impediments to the free flow of consciousness. Just as a light from a room is obscured by a dirty window and when you clean the window the light shines brightly.

The quality of your action depends upon the quality of your thinking

Without thinking, there is no activity. If your thoughts are weak then the actions that arise from those thoughts will lack power. If your thoughts are strong and clear, then the activity that comes from them will be effective and successful.

The quality and efficacy of your actions and thoughts are a function of how conscious you are.

The light of consciousness

We cannot solve our problems with the same level of thinking that created them.

Albert Einstein

Imagine a totally darkened room full of people. They're trying to live and work, yet they can't see where they're going. They keep bumping into each other and tripping over objects, resulting in conflict, mistakes and a lack of productivity.

Finally someone steps up and assumes a leadership role. They suggest forming a committee to launch an inquiry to get to the bottom of the problem. How best to rearrange the furniture? How should they organise themselves so they don't keep getting bruised and knocked about? Do they need to invent a device to warn them when they're getting too close?

Then someone new enters the room and turns on the light. In an instant everyone can see what's going on. They can communicate more effectively and so avoid danger and mishaps. A simple action with a transformational effect. By introducing a second element, the situation is transformed.

Turning on the light is like increasing consciousness. Become more aware. Be more perceptive. Stop working at the level of the problem. Don't waste time reinventing the wheel. Instead, step beyond the issue by bringing the light of consciousness to the situation and then the darkness of ignorance will go.

Consciousness is the basis of everything

We have to recognise that we are spiritual beings with souls existing in a spiritual world as well as material beings with bodies and brains existing in a material world.

Sir John Eccles, Nobel Prize-winning neurophysiologist

The Veda – 'pure knowledge' or 'truth' – is an ancient body of knowledge that reveals the nature of life. This universal knowledge is many thousands of years old and yet contains time-less wisdom for the modern age. The ancient Vedic masters were able to cognise the most fundamental truth of existence. They discovered that underlying the finite boundaries of everything in creation is a wholeness that is unbounded and infinite. Everything that exists in the physical world is a manifestation of a field of energy that holds the potential to create anything and everything.

The wise sages of the Veda sum it up in this way:

I am That, Thou art That, All this is That

All the laws of nature, and all form and phenomena, come from this one, indivisible, whole field of creative energy and intelli-gence. The Vedas state that there is no separation between you and this field – this is your *essential* nature. While not visible at the surface layer, it can be experienced beyond the normal thinking level, transcendent and silent. The more you experi-ence your essence, the more you identify with your true Self. In waking up this background silence by stepping beyond the body and mind, the transcendent ceases to be transcendent. The direct experience of this silence is the gift of meditation. As a result, the fountainhead of creation comes alive and embeds itself in all your thinking and actions.

In the Vedas there are many names for this field:
the Self, Being, the Absolute, samadhi, pure consciousness, pure awareness, transcendental consciousness, OM, a field of creative intelligence.

What does this mean for us?
- The source of everything in the universe is one whole, indivisible field of energy – Being.
- Being is omnipresent – it is all form and phenomena, everywhere, at all times.
- Everything we perceive is a spontaneous manifestation from the source.
- Consciousness unifies everything and everyone.
- At our source we're all made of the same stuff.
- In our essential, least excited state, we're all connected.

Waves on the ocean might look separate and defined, but they're all made of the same stuff. The seawater in one wave is the same seawater as the next wave and the next. You are not separate. You're not just some isolated mass of muscle and bones making your way through the world. You are one with everything.

Ancient wisdom meets modern science

I regard consciousness as fundamental.
I regard matter as derivative from consciousness...
Everything that we talk about, everything that we regard
as existing, postulates consciousness.

Max Planck, theoretical physicist, originator of quantum theory

Leading-edge science is validating the ancient Vedic perspective of the reality of life. The most important insights are emerging from quantum physics, the most accurate branch of science investigating the subtlest aspects of nature.

The Unified Field theory first began to be developed in the late 1800s and has evolved to be one of the most fascinating studies in science. In the twentieth century, this exploration into the deeper, quantum layers of reality has revealed a deeper truth.

Energy is the basis of everything

The materialist Newtonian model of particles bumping into each like billiard balls has been replaced by an understanding of the interconnected nature of all existence. Physicists have discovered that at the most fundamental level, there is only one thing. Energy is the basis of everything in the universe. Niels Bohr, one of the founders of quantum theory, declared: 'Everything we call real is made of things that cannot be regarded as real.'

The idea, as generally agreed, goes like this:

At the surface, material layer of life, matter is made up of molecules. All molecules are composed of two or more smaller structures, atoms. Atoms consist of a nucleus (protons and neutrons) surrounded by a cloud of electrons. These subatomic particles are comprised of elementary particles such as bosons, leptons and quarks. However, these building blocks are not actually particles. They're localised, condensed wave forms, fluctuating on an underlying non-material field.

As a quark's wave function rises and falls rapidly, it begins to take on the appearance of structure. Quarks and leptons arrange themselves into electrons, protons and neutrons. These sub-atomic particles then build the atoms, which combine to form molecules – the 'stuff' we see and interact with. Yet all that stuff is built of non-material, energetic waves.

As Fritjof Capra writes in his book, *The Tao of Physics*:

Quantum theory thus reveals a basic oneness of the universe. It shows that we cannot decompose the world into independently existing smallest units. As we penetrate into matter, nature does not show us any isolated 'building blocks,' but rather appears as a complicated web of relations between the various parts of the whole.

Solid matter appears solid only at a level that our senses are able to perceive. However, things that we interact with at the macro level are not, at their source, things. They are energy. That baseline from which they emerge is one, whole, indivisible field of energy. Physics calls this the Unified Field. Everything is arising from this. Everything *is* this.

An intelligent universe

Mathematics and beauty are the foundation stones of the universe. No one who has studied the forces of nature can doubt that the world about us is a manifestation of something very, very clever indeed.

Paul Davies, physicist

The Unified Field doesn't manifest randomly. It is organised. It displays intelligent coordination between seemingly disparate parts. It exhibits precise patterns that obey laws of nature that have been modelled by mathematical theory – elegantly complex formulae to demonstrate how these laws unfold with astounding accuracy.

The ground state of creation gives rise to all the laws of nature – intelligent and orderly expressions of nature that govern existence.

Consciousness is primary

And so we come full circle to the ancient Vedic discoveries about the essence of life. Science tells us there's only one thing. And we know that consciousness exists. Therefore, that one thing must be conscious. And every 'thing' that arises from it is also conscious. I'm conscious, you're conscious, a sunflower moving in sync with the sun is conscious. I am That, Thou art That, All this is That.

Consciousness is primary, and all physical matter is created out of a process of the intelligent, unfolding patterns of nature.

Different states of consciousness

Sleeping, dreaming and waking

Prior to learning to meditate, we're very familiar with three states of consciousness: sleeping, dreaming and waking. Each state has its own measurable mode of physiological functioning, and each generates a very different experience of reality.

In waking state your heart rate, metabolic rate and blood chemistry will reflect the level of activity within a particular range. Your brain functioning will also indicate a wakeful pattern as measured on an electroencephalogram.

During deep sleep, you're not aware of yourself or other objects and your body rests. The body automatically repairs, balances hormones and biochemistry, and processes the experiences of the day into memories. Heart rate decreases, metabolic rate drops and brain-wave patterns change, creating another distinct psychophysiological signature.

During dreaming there is a set of brain-wave patterns, rapid eye movements (REM), muscular relaxation and increased metabolic rate that are different to what's observed in wakefulness or sleep. As tension from the day is normalised, mental and physical activity increase, and you become aware of changing dream images.

A fourth state of consciousness

In meditation there's a fourth state of consciousness that can be experienced with its own psychophysiological signature. The Vedic texts refer to this as *turiya*, which means 'the fourth'.

The fourth, say the wise, is the pure Self, alone.
Dwelling in the heart of all, It is the lord of all, the seer of all,
*   the source and goal of all.*
It is not outer awareness. It is not inner awareness, nor is It a
*   suspension of awareness.*
It is not knowing. It is not unknowing, nor is it Knowingness itself.
It can neither be seen nor understood.
It cannot be given boundaries.
It is ineffable and beyond thought.
It is indefinable.
It is known only through becoming It.
It is the end of all activity, silent and unchanging, the supreme
*   good, one without a second.*
It is the real Self.
It, above all, should be known.

The Upanishads, translated by Alistair Shearer (with Peter Russell)

In an automatic self-transcending style of meditation, there are periods during the practice where you experience no mantra and no thought. The mantra becomes fainter and fainter to the point that it's almost imperceptible. Then it disappears, and for a moment no thought comes to replace it. The mind falls mute; however, the meditator isn't asleep. They're awake, highly alert and yet without thoughts. In this state of least-excitation, the meditator has 'stepped beyond' or transcended thinking to arrive at the source of thought itself. This is the experience of *turiya*, the fourth state of consciousness.

A state of restful alertness

We can measure these transcendent moments. All the markers of activity in the brain and body indicate something very different is going on than in the other three states. Metabolic rate drops significantly, heart rate slows down, production of stress chemistry reduces, relaxation levels increase and the brain becomes highly coherent and orderly. This is why this state is often referred to as a state of 'restful alertness': the body is resting deeply and yet the brain is alert and fully aware. These physiological and biochemical markers indicate a state of consciousness that is distinct from sleeping, dreaming and waking.

These moments are not random; they are experienced regularly and systematically. Rather than merely being a feel-good mood, they're a natural, routine experience that's had in every meditation sitting. When your mind can regularly experience that least-excited state, you begin to expand the degree to which you have that pure value of consciousness.

This state is the source of your energy, intelligence, creativity, compassion and happiness. By touching this state of restful alertness, these qualities are enlivened and engaged in all aspects of your life. The meditator comes out of meditation and transports these qualities into all their thinking and activity. They feel intellectually sharper, mentally refreshed, physically energised, psychologically balanced and emotionally more stable.

The power of the present moment

I'm often asked: 'Is there a difference between meditation and mindfulness?'

These are very different practices.

Let's start with what it means to be mindful. Here's a definition from the mindfulness app, Headspace:

Mindfulness is the quality of being present and fully engaged with whatever we're doing at the moment – free from distraction or judgement, and aware of our thoughts and feelings without getting caught up in them.

The description of this state is a good one. All these qualities are desirable. But how does one get there?

I know many mindfulness practitioners who describe a variety of different approaches. Some are done while walking, others sitting quietly and others are practised while engaged in an activity, like washing the dishes. They all involve monitoring whatever's happening with the aim of *staying in the present moment*. Notice how the body feels, the contact point of the feet with the ground, the feel of the air on the skin, watch the breath and observe thoughts as they float through the mind. Try not to drift into the past or begin planning and speculating about the future.

While this all sounds good, people who try it often report it being hard work.

It takes effort to hold the attention in this way. Thoughts may settle down to some degree, but the mind is still thinking. Without a systematic, effortless dive to the least excited state of consciousness, the mind and the body remain more engaged and less deeply rested.

This is very different to the automatic self-transcending practice that I have been describing. Rather than being a practice of trying to stay in the moment, we remove the obstructions (i.e. stress and tiredness) that block our capacity to be fully awake and present. Then, having dissolved those blockages during meditation, you come out more able to perceive what's actually going on. You're more mindful. In this way, present moment awareness is an *outcome* of meditation.

Felicity sums this up beautifully:

> *I find it so hard to describe the effect meditating has on my life. It is subtle, intangible and beautiful. Twice a day one goes to an extraordinary place of calm. Meditating is a love affair: colours are brighter, food tastes more delicious, my equilibrium recovers more quickly after being accosted by aggression or bad news. If I go into the world, and I haven't meditated that day, something feels distinctly wrong, like leaving the house without cleaning my teeth!*

starter tip

Come to Your Senses

So often we're stressed and out of sorts because we're worried about the past or the future – two things we have no control over. Rehashing yesterday or rehearsing tomorrow takes our attention and energy away from the here and now.

Your five senses – hearing, sight, smell, taste and touch – are the gateway into the present moment. One of the best ways to re-engage in the present is to literally 'come to your senses'. Here's a quick and easy exercise to do just that:

- Sit or stand and take a moment to get comfortable.
- Tune into the sense of sound. Take twenty seconds and note the noises around you – loud and subtle, near and far.
- Now move to the sense of sight. Take twenty seconds and note what you can see around you – colours, texture, light and shadow.
- Next take twenty seconds to note what aromas you detect – food, perfume, humidity in the air.
- Then take twenty seconds to note the various tastes in your mouth – toothpaste, coffee, chewing gum.
- Finally, move on to the sense of touch. Take twenty seconds and note what you feel – the textures of your clothes, the temperature of the air, the weight of your limbs.

By taking a few moments to wake up each of the senses, you return to what's actually happening in the present moment. It is from this place of alertness that you regain your spark and enjoyment for life.

Why do I need a technique?

Automatic self-transcending meditation is an easy, effortless technique.

You're not training your mind to experience something new or different. Often when I teach someone to meditate, in their very first meditation, they'll say something like: 'I've felt this before' or 'I feel like I've come home'.

There's something very familiar about experiencing this quiet state, even if it's not an explicit memory. As we've seen, the innermost aspect of one's self is a universal aspect of everyone and everything. Pure consciousness or Being is the basis of all existence – including you.

So an obvious question arises. If this is so universal, natural and blissful, why do we need to learn a technique to experience it? Why don't we experience it naturally?

Swimming is natural. And you still have to learn how to do it. Just because something is natural doesn't mean you don't need to develop the skill of how to do it.

Meditation is not producing an experience that's new or created in some way. Rather, it's delivering access to something that ordinarily gets overshadowed by the busyness and activity of life.

The mind is naturally pulled into thinking and action by the senses of perception. Society teaches us from a young age to find satisfaction via this world of sensory experience. You're attracted and stimulated by what you see, hear, taste, smell and touch in your environment. But there is no encouragement and no training in how to experience subtlety and silence within. Without this, the mind misses its own, essential nature. Constantly drawn to action, it fails to know itself. The more the senses are bombarded with gross levels of mental activity, the less able we are to appreciate the finer layers. Those subtle, inner aspects cease to be detectable.

The mind needs a method for turning away from thinking and doing to dive inwards. This is the value of meditation.

Different techniques emphasise different levels

As we've discussed, not all meditation and relaxation techniques are the same. The mechanics of the different styles are different and the results and benefits vary considerably.

Most notably, the starting point for these different techniques varies. For example, it's not that a body-led practice doesn't have an effect on the mind and consciousness. It's a question of what's the primary level of impact.

Here are some examples of meditation and relaxation techniques arranged accordingly:

Starting Point	Physical Engagement
Action / Body	Chanting
	Hatha yoga
	Breathing techniques
	Walking
	Qigong
	Tai Chi

Starting Point	Concentration and Open Monitoring
Thinking / Mind	Tibetan Buddhism
	Prayer
	Mindfulness
	Vipassana
	Guided meditation
	Visualisation

Starting Point	Auto Self-Transcending
Being / Pure Consciousness	*Vedic Meditation*
	Transcendental Meditation
	Primordial Sound Meditation
	Art of Living: Sahaj Samadhi Meditation

WHY MEDITATE?

When I first explored meditation, I was looking for change – a positive upgrade to how I was feeling and behaving. If you'd asked me why I was learning to meditate I'd have said I wanted more energy, less anxiety and to feel healthier. I was after clear, tangible improvements.

It's often these kinds of practical upgrades people are looking for. Things like getting better sleep, feeling less anxious, experiencing more clarity and a sense of feeling calm and grounded.

Fortunately, there's an abundance of evidence that meditation will address these desires. We'll be going into a lot of detail about this shortly.

And there's a deeper, more profound aspect to wanting to learn.

I don't think I was capable of articulating what I was truly looking for when I first came to meditation. There was a more fundamental desire that lay behind my search and it's an insight that becomes more evident over time, as you build the daily practice into your life.

With hindsight and many years of meditation, I can look back on myself as a young, stressed woman and see more clearly. On the surface, I was doing okay. I was healthy, had a good job and was having lots of nice experiences. But I wasn't feeling genuinely, deeply happy. I wasn't sure of myself. I didn't feel I was making the most of my life. I had a sense time was racing by, even though I was only in my twenties. And I knew I wanted this to shift.

Here are some deeper reasons why you might be considering meditation:

- You're enjoying success in certain areas and yet have a sense there's something more.

- You can see parts of your life that are unsustainable (health, eating habits or sleep).
- You've spent years achieving and acquiring, but are not feeling peaceful or happy.
- Your emotional state is clouded by anxiety, resentment or deep sadness.
- You feel stuck, gripped by indecision, lacking a sense of purpose.
- Relationships feel strained or empty.
- Something about your life just doesn't feel right.

If any of this resonates, you're reading the right book. And you're not alone.

Passing the 'So What' test

How you spend your time is very important. As I've mentioned, time is the most valuable resource you have.

If you're going to invest your time sitting around with your eyes closed meditating, you need to:

a) want to do it
b) see a return on that investment

This is where the 'So What' test comes in.

There's so much talk about how meditation is a good thing. However, it needs to be more than simply a nice-sounding thing to do. You need to be able to answer the question: *So what will meditating each day actually do for me?*

10 Reasons to Meditate

This is where we get to the heart of *Why Meditate?*

There are many reasons why people come to meditation. Whatever you're after, the benefits are cumulative. Upgrades to your life don't come in isolation – positive change in one area will initiate change in many others.

I've grouped these benefits into ten key reasons why meditation is one of the most valuable tools to build into your life.

Less stress

Less stress

Why we need to talk about stress

In looking at the many reasons to meditate it makes sense to start with stress. Stress is the precursor to much of the suffering in the world today. I would go as far as to say it's the number-one reason people are unwell, unhappy and behaving in ways that are harmful to themselves and others. In short, chronic stress leads to sickness, misery and bad decisions.

In my lectures on meditation, I talk a lot about stress and the effect it has on emotional and physical well-being. Often, I'm asked 'What's the best way to manage stress?' I quickly respond: 'I'm not into *managing* stress. I'm into *eliminating* stress.' Managing implies that it's something we have to cope with and, therefore, learn to live with. As if it's a given that we're going to accumulate stress throughout our lives. At best, we have to learn to put up with it and develop tactics to keep stress from wearing us down and making us sick.

This is not my starting point. You don't have to be on the back foot when it comes to stress. You don't have to be in a reactive state where your normal daily experience is bound by the limitations of living with chronic tension. I want to raise the bar so that you have a natural way to *eliminate* stress rather than merely manage it. I want you to get ahead of the game and have a tool that allows you to release stress faster than you gain it.

This is the point of meditation

Living in this rapidly changing world means we're all subjected to demands we weren't dealing with even a few decades ago.

In the 1970s, the average person saw 500 to 1,600 ads per day. Most ads were on billboards, in newspapers and on TV. Fast-forward to 2020 and the digital age. Now the average person encounters 6,000 to 10,000 ads every single day. This is a 600 per cent increase in the space of five decades. And this is only advertising. In this social media age, the number of messages you see in one 24-hour period is mind-boggling.

And even this is just a fraction of what we have to respond to. Technological advancements affect every area of our lives – we're moving faster, communicating more quickly and innovating at breakneck speed.

How we respond to these demands will determine how much we're affected by stress. The question is not whether you will experience stress in your life. You will. Stress is a universal human experience. The more important questions are: Will you store that stress in your system? Will your behaviours and choices be bound by it? Will you be physically and emotionally limited by it? Or will you have a way of releasing it from your system?

The fight-or-flight response

The evolution of the human body is relatively slow. Physically, we're much the same as we were 100,000 years ago. But our minds, our knowledge of the world and ability to manipulate the environment, are changing at increasingly faster rates. It's as if we're living in a 21st-century environment with minds to match, and yet our bodies really haven't changed since the Stone Age.

Stress is not a new phenomenon in terms of our development as human beings. Humans have always had to respond to danger and are hard-wired to react swiftly. This reaction has been crucial to the survival of the human race.

In the 1930s the American physiologist Walter Cannon was the first to coin the phrase *'fight-or-flight'*. Cannon realised that a chain of internal reactions mobilised the body's resources to deal with threatening circumstances. He argued that fear and anger have served as preparation for action and have developed over time as a central part of our existence. 'Fear has become associated with the instinct to run, to escape; and anger or aggressive feeling, with the instinct to attack. These are fundamental emotions and instincts.'

What happens in the moment of fight-or-flight?

Let's go back 15,000 years to when your ancestors were trekking through the woods and came face to face with a mountain lion. Their lives depended on how they responded to that threat and instantly the fight-or-flight response kicked in. They either had to fight the danger, or get out of there fast.

When danger is sensed, immediately a message is sent to the brain via the amygdala. The amygdala is the part of the brain that processes emotions, including fear. It sends a distress signal to the hypothalamus, which is like the command centre. The hypothalamus communicates with the rest of the body via the autonomic nervous system, which controls involuntary functions like breathing, blood pressure and heartbeat. The sympathetic nervous system is triggered and the fight-or-flight response is activated, providing a burst of energy so that the body can respond to perceived danger.

The adrenal glands begin pumping stress hormones like norepinephrine into the bloodstream. The heart beats faster to push blood to the muscles and vital organs so you can move quickly.

Blood pressure rises. Blood vessels in the skin constrict and clots form to minimise blood loss. Small airways in the lungs open wide so you can take in as much oxygen as possible. Extra oxygen is sent to the brain, increasing alertness. Pupils dilate to allow more light into the eyes. Sight, hearing and other senses become sharper.

Meanwhile, norepinephrine triggers the release of blood sugar (glucose). Nutrients flood into the bloodstream, supplying energy to all parts of the body. If danger continues to be perceived then the pituitary gland triggers a cascade of more stress hormones and the adrenal glands release cortisol to keep the body revved up and on high alert.

And while all this is happening, there are many other vital functions that are interrupted and put on hold. It's like there's a message from the captain saying 'We're under attack – mobilise all energy to deal with this danger!'

One example is the digestive system, which becomes compromised as blood and oxygen flow to the stomach drops. Digestion slows down, or even stops, which can result in imbalance and inflammation in the stomach and intestines.

Likewise, the fight-or-flight response affects your immune system, which is constantly performing hundreds of vital functions. Normally, it's scanning for bacteria, viruses, parasites and overproduction of cells. However, when the mind and body detect danger, the immune system changes its priorities to address the most immediate threat. Not cancer, not tapeworm, not a cold. Instead, the immune system prepares for things like a bacterial incursion. If you're being attacked by a predator, an injury could result in infection. So, the whole system reorients itself to fight that potential threat.

All these reactions happen quickly and automatically.

Let's say our ancestors dealt with the mountain lion and were able to fight or flee, unscathed. They got to play out the fight-or-flight response that was needed in that moment. Once it was over they recovered from the acute stress and returned to a state of balance.

Now fast-forward 15,000 years.

The fight-or-flight stress response is a very different story today. Imagine you're driving to an important job interview. The traffic is terrible because there's been an accident and you're running late. You didn't sleep well last night and you had a rough start to the day when your toddler didn't want to be dropped at nursery. There's no way you're getting there in time and you're starting to feel anxious. In that moment, the fight-or-flight response kicks in. Heart rate and blood pressure rise. Acid starts dumping into your stomach to get rid of breakfast because digestion is not a priority right now. You want to urinate because your body thinks it needs to be light and nimble. Stress chemicals are flooding your bloodstream, keeping you on high alert. Your immune system begins to change its priorities away from fighting viruses and dealing with overproduction of cells. Antibodies course through your system to prepare for a potential bacterial incursion in case you get bitten.

There's no lion in the car, but your body doesn't know it. It perceives a threat and all those same reactions are activated – most often without you even being aware they're happening. In that heightened state of excitation your system is responding in a way that is out of sync with the demand you're facing. However, as much as you might understand that intellectually, in that moment the executive processing part of your brain is not engaged. The frontal lobes in the brain go offline, leaving you hyper-alert and yet without a sense of the larger context. Rational thinking is not available and you're reacting in a way that's neither appropriate nor healthy. You get tunnel vision and lose perspective.

Now imagine the rest of your day. You eventually arrive at your interview late. You do the interview, still feeling wound up and frazzled because of the traffic. You haven't yet recovered from the previous demand and now you're facing another challenge. More stress. More fight-or-flight reactivity. The interview doesn't go so well and you leave feeling tense and angry. When you pick up your child from nursery you're still feeling off, and you end up being snappy and impatient. More stress. More fight-or-flight reactions in the body. And so it continues in a downward spiral.

Acute stress becomes chronic stress

Often stress is linked to isolated peak moments of demand, such as loss of a loved one or the breakdown of a close relationship. While these sudden, intense demands are strong sources of stress, it's more often the relentless, fast-paced demands of everyday life that build up over time.

Stress is at epidemic levels in our society. Unlike our ancestors we will rarely, if ever, have to deal with a moment where we have to physically fight or flee for our life. However we will face many, many demands – even in one 24-hour period. And these small, repeating incidents lead to a state of chronic stress in daily life.

There's a negative feedback loop at play here. If you're unable to meet a demand appropriately you have a stress reaction.

You're thrown out of balance and your ability to meet the next demand goes down. Then you can't handle the new demand because you haven't yet recovered from the previous one, so more stress is gained. And so it goes on.

Living life in a state of permanent stress reaction is not good for us. It will negatively impact all aspects of life, including your health, decision making, rate of ageing, ability to deal with change and the quality of your relationships.

What is stress?

It's important we get very clear about what stress is. It's a word that's crept into common parlance in a way that can be misleading. Often stress is thought of as an emotional response – nervous tension and agitation – in the face of demands. However, rather than being solely a subjective feeling, stress is a set of physiological events in the body that are measurable and verifiable.

The Hungarian-Canadian endocrinologist Hans Selye was the first to use the term stress in terms of how humans respond to demands. In his book *Stress Without Distress*, Selye defined stress as 'The non-specific response of the body to any demand made upon it.' He went on to say '…it is immaterial whether the agent or situation we face is pleasant or unpleasant.'

Let's break this down so we understand the most important aspects of stress:

- All demands have one thing in common – they ask us to adapt. And we adapt in a way that is general and non-specific, irrespective of what the demand is. It might be a loud noise, or a sudden temperature change, a bacterial infection or a winning lotto ticket. A demanding physical or emotional event will trigger the same general reaction in the body's defences. This reaction is what Selye called stress. The event that triggers this reaction is called a stressor.

- Demands can be physical or psychological. Physical factors include things like lack of sleep, loud noise, drugs, intense heat or cold. Psychological factors include the threat of physical harm, a demanding job (or a boring job!), divorce, grief, highly competitive environments, and lack of emotional safety and love.
- Stress begins with a mental attitude about the nature of a demand. The mind is responsible for the body moving into a stress reaction. However, stress does not *reside* in the mind. Stress is a body response. We can measure what's happening in the brain, hormonal system, immune system and various internal organs of someone who is stressed. Even though we might experience it emotionally, it's not simply affecting the mind.
- You can be stressed without feeling it, without any awareness of these bodily changes playing out in your system.
- Stress is not limited to 'negative' demands. Selye gives the example of a mother suffering a sudden mental shock when told her son has died in battle. When years later he walks into her room, alive and well, she experiences extreme joy. While the specific nature of the events are in opposition – grief and joy – the stressor effect – the non-specific demand to readjust to a new situation – may be the same.
- Stress is both an overreaction to an initial demand *and* the way the body stores the memory of that overreaction. These memories of the overreaction are stored in the cells of the body and become stress triggers in the future.

The binding effect of stress

When you have multiple, ongoing stress experiences, your body begins to habituate the stress response in the face of demands. Then the body begins to programme into it what that situation was and all the circumstances around it. We call these stress memories *premature cognitive commitments*, or PCCs.

A study carried out in the late 1970s looked at stress in teenage boys while they were watching TV. When advertisements for a certain type of car came on, loud alarms went off. In those moments the boys' stress levels rose significantly. Then the boys were monitored while watching TV without any stress-inducing noise being imposed. Even in the absence of the alarming noise, every time the car advertisement appeared, the boys' stress levels rose massively.

Why? You get stressed once and the brain associates that stress event with everything that's in the environment *in that moment*. Whatever you're tasting, seeing, hearing, smelling, touching in that moment is being memorised by the brain. These experiences are then embedded as triggers for a stress response. These are what psychologists mean when they refer to PCCs.

If in the future one of those factors is present, then the body will automatically be triggered into a stress reaction. This means these triggers are dictating your body's reaction to demands, rather than the reality of the present moment.

Imagine you had an unpleasant experience once and there was some incense burning in the background. Two years later, someone lights that same incense and you start to feel jumpy and nervous and you don't know why. Intellectually it doesn't make sense – everything in that present moment is fine. However, your body doesn't know that. It's bound by a memory that's been stored in the cells of the body. No amount of intellectual analysis will be able to override the body's response.

a word about:

Stressful Situations

It's important to make a distinction between the trigger for a stress reaction and the nature of the reaction itself. A stressor is the scientific term for the demands we face in life. These are potential triggers that may or may not set off a stress reaction. The key word is 'potential'.

Often I'll hear people say 'Lunch with my in-laws is so stressful.' Or 'Monday management meetings with my boss are stressful.' These statements imply that it's the situation that is responsible for making someone stressed.

There's no such thing as a stressful situation. There are only stressful responses to given situations.

Situations can be demanding and challenging. People can be difficult. There may be jobs you'd rather not do. However it's not the situation, person or job that determines whether you get stressed or not.

Two people might be in the same meeting. One person's getting stressed and the other is not. It's the response to the situation that determines whether someone has a stress reaction, not the situation itself.

There's also a positive alternative. If you're able to interact with a stressor successfully, it will lead to a wave of joy. Demands in and of themselves do not equal stress. Stress is a response, and almost invariably, it's a response that damages your nervous system.

Stress is the result of overload

Stress comes about due to a combination of pressure, overload and excitation, and an inability to recover. Let's take the simple example of a rubber band. If you apply pressure and stretch the band, it changes shape. For a moment it's distorted compared to its original state. When you remove the pressure, if it goes back to a state of balance, we call that structure elastic. It has recovered from the overload of experience and resumed its original state. This balance state is called homeostasis – the ability to maintain internal orderliness and stability, in the presence of changes in the external environment.

However, if a structure is subject to ongoing pressure, overload and excitation and the build-up of distortion is such that the structure can't return to an original state of balance, it's no longer fully elastic. The overloading experiences have left an imprint.

This is exactly what's happening in the body when it's exposed to repeated demands and isn't able to fully recover. The overloading experience leaves an impression on the physiology – the body has accumulated stress.

How does meditation help reduce stress?

The good news is we can do something about this accumulation of stress. There's a big difference between *getting* stressed and *staying* stressed. If given the chance, the body will automatically dissolve accumulated tensions and return to a state of homeostasis. Deep rest is the state that allows for this recovery.

Rest as the antidote to stress

A build-up of stress occurs when there is too much excitation of the mind and no systematic approach to resting the body. We need to find a way to turn off the amygdala and de-excite. In our modern world, sleep is not delivering enough rest to keep ahead of the game. We end up gaining stress faster than we can release it. This is where meditation changes the equation. If you're resting more deeply than when sleeping, you release stress more quickly.

Reduction in stress hormones

Much of the brain's control of the body is via hormones – chemical messengers travelling around the body, activating and deactivating various organs and cells. One of the ways we can measure the level of stress in a person is by looking at the changes in the stress hormones flooding their system. Chronic stress results in our bodies being in a state of high alert in response to demands that actually don't present a real danger to our physical bodies.

In those situations, the body releases a toxic cocktail of stress hormones that cannot be properly metabolised. Two of the big hitters in this hormonal blast are norepinephrine and cortisol. What we see in meditators is that cortisol levels go down. The adrenal glands stop pumping out norepinephrine and the body is in a state of 'stay-and-play' rather than 'fight-or-flight'.

Stress comes in different flavours

While stress is a physiological distortion, the effects are commonly felt emotionally. In my work, I see three main types or 'flavours' of stress that people experience when they're feeling stressed. There are of course variations on these three; however, they represent the core emotions that tend to manifest. With each of these, there's a continuum from mild to very intense expressions of the feeling.

Fear – this ranges from some little, niggly worries through to terror and panic.

Anger – feeling a bit cranky and irritable, through to full-blown rage.
Sadness – feeling a bit hurty-poos about something, through to deep, dark depression.

In addition to these, I see a lot of agitation and impatience, which manifests as jumpiness in the body or a feeling of being mentally very scattered and unable to focus. I think lots of screen time has a part to play here. And the tendency for many people to be doing too much – racing around, long days, lots of external stimulation – it all contributes. Interestingly, the more stressed and worn out you become, the harder it is to settle. This is why so many people are struggling to sleep (more on that in a bit).

We can do something about it

Stress causes you to do the opposite of whatever's needed in a situation. It makes you aggressive and pushy, when you need to step back and listen. It makes you lethargic and slow, when you need to step up and be on the front foot. The good news is you can do something about it. Rather than being defined by your stress, you can start to feel better about yourself. Stress can be dissolved when you know how to rest deeply.

starter tip

Body Feeling Technique

As we've seen, stress is a body-based experience. The following technique is a simple way to begin to release stress by deliberately tuning in to the language of sensation in your body.

When the body is holding tension, there will be a sensation somewhere in the physiology. By bringing your awareness to these places of tension we facilitate release, just like unwinding a knot in a rope.

Sit easily, close the eyes and take a moment to get comfortable.

- Bring your attention to any sensations in the body.
- Somewhere there will be a dominant sensation. It might be anything – tightness in the chest; a tingle on top of the head; even an itch in the big toe.
- Gently bring the attention to that sensation. There is no need to concentrate or focus – simply let the attention lightly rest there and witness the feeling in the body.
- After a moment, that sensation will start to shift and dissolve. Another sensation will become primary.
- Let the attention move to this new sensation and location – a twinge in the hip from yesterday's exercise; a tightness in the back of the neck; or a feeling of lightness in the stomach.
- Again after a few moments this will begin to dissipate and another part of the body will draw your attention. Continue in just the same way.
- After just a few minutes, you'll naturally find yourself thinking other thoughts easily – almost a sense of daydreaming. Open the eyes slowly.

This simple exercise allows the body to settle down so we can tune in to what's happening in that moment. When the body stops preparing for fight-or-flight, we can move into stay-and-play and operate from our most engaged and creative state.

Calm in the face of change

Calm in the face of change

I'm writing this in September 2020, six months into a pandemic. The amount of change everyone has dealt with would have been unimaginable a year ago. But the truth is, change is always happening. It is the constant in life – relationships, careers, economies, governments, our very planet – always changing.

Your own body is a perfect example of this constant flux. The body replaces itself with a completely new set of cells every seven to ten years. Some cells change in just a few days. You'll have a new stomach lining within five days. Skin cells rejuvenate every two to four weeks. The cells in your liver will be renewed every five to sixteen months. Your bones take a bit longer, although they'll be fully renewed within ten years. Your body today is very different to the body you had last year. Change is the one constant in life.

Everything and everyone is changing – at all times

Our ability to adapt to change is central to how we experience life. Removing demands and simplifying your life is only possible up to a point. You can declutter, opt out and slow down to some extent; however, it's not possible to remove all demands. While the idea of running away to live in a tree house on a hippie commune might seem appealing, it doesn't remove the chance of you getting stressed. When the roof on the tree house starts to leak, you might experience as much stress as the Wall Street trader who just lost $20 million.

Demands are an opportunity for adaptation

When someone says, 'A little bit of stress is good for you,' what they're really saying is that pressures, challenges and deadlines are good for you. I agree. Experiencing demands is good because it stimulates growth and creativity. Meet a challenge successfully, and you'll enjoy the waves of fulfilment that come as a result.

Demands do not necessarily equal stress; although for one person a demand may be experienced as stress, for another it may be seen as a challenge. When we cannot meet a challenge and adapt to it, our system gets overwhelmed and that is when we get stressed.

While not all demands are as demanding as others, they all ask something of you. **A demand is a change in expectation.** It's new information. You thought the train was going to arrive in ten minutes and it's half an hour. You expected your toddler to fall asleep before 8 p.m. and at 9.30 p.m. you're still reading stories. You thought your client was going to pay on time and now you have bills due. Each of these situations asks you to pivot. You thought it was going a certain way and it shifts. New information demands a new response and this takes energy.

If you manage to change gears and adapt to new information, then you enjoy success and the satisfaction that follows. If instead, you maladapt and you're unable to come up with an *appropriate* response, you experience stress. Demands don't equal stress. Maladaptation to a demand leads to stress.

a word about:

Appropriate vs Nice

I use the word appropriate very specifically. The appropriate response is different in every situation. There are no rules about what is appropriate. One response may be to say nothing. Another situation might require someone to step up and be quite forceful. For meditators it's not about always trying to manufacture some mood of smiley niceness. The most appropriate response may require you to be very direct and play a corrective role with someone. The key is to be flexible and aware, to meet the demand in a way that improves and upgrades, rather than creating more tension and stress.

Adaptability is key

Resistance is futile.

The Borg, *Star Trek: The Next Generation*

Whatever you resist in life persists. Trying to stop things and people from changing is like trying to stop a river from flowing. It won't work and it will be a bruising process. Resisting the ever-changing nature of life will always lead to suffering. This is why adaptability is one of the greatest skills we can develop. As Hans Selye says in his book *Stress Without Distress*: 'Adaptability is probably the most distinctive characteristic of life.'

The 'father of stress research', Selye, identified a three-stage response in the body to stress, which he called the 'General Adaptation Syndrome'. The first stage is the *Alarm* stage (fight-or-flight reaction), where there is an initial hyper-excitatory reaction to the demand. When you're under prolonged stress you enter the second stage of *Resistance* – your body is no longer in alarm and begins to relax. While it might look like you've successfully adapted to the stressor, this is not the case. It's simply that the effects of stress are continually sapping your strength, just as the light of the torch gets dimmer if you leave it on all the time. Then the third stage is the stage of *Exhaustion*, which Selye termed *'a kind of premature ageing due to wear and tear…'*. This is when adaptation energy is depleted, and the symptoms of alarm return.

Think of your adaptation capacity like a bank account – your Adaptation Energy balance. If your Adaptation Energy balance is in the black, with lots of zeros on the end, you've got plenty to draw down upon. When a change in expectation comes along, you're able to meet it without being drained and thrown off course.

But if your Adaptation Energy bank balance is in overdraft, meeting a demand is going to be tough. You don't have the energy to draw down upon to meet the change. You end up over or underreacting, and gaining stress. If you come under more stress while you're in the stage of Resistance, your ability to adapt drops dramatically. Then the exhaustion stage sets in even more rapidly.

This is where meditation is so powerful

Without adequate rest and recovery mechanisms, the body's capacity to adapt is finite. However, every time you meditate it's as if you're topping up your Adaptation Energy bank balance. Because meditation gives you energy. Think of Adaptation Energy like a buffer zone between you and the demand. It gives you the ability to be on the front foot and stay calm and responsive in the face of change. It gives you the space to see the broadest possible view of what's going on.

This is one of the things I noticed very early on when I started meditating. Before meditation, life felt like being in a small boat in the middle of a huge storm. I had so much going on with work and other challenges, it felt like I was being tossed around by the waves and wind. In truth I felt like I was about to sink, or crash onto the rocks. I was overwhelmed by everything I had to deal with.

When I started meditating it was as if someone put the anchor overboard. I was staying above the waves rather than being swamped by them. It wasn't like the storm miraculously stopped once I began meditating – I still had a lot going on in my life – however, I was no longer feeling at the mercy of it all. And the biggest change I noticed was that things that previously would have thrown me no longer knocked me off-balance. I was handling things differently. I didn't feel as overwhelmed all the time and my responses were way more effective.

One of my students, Ellie, shares the transformative effect meditation has had on dealing with huge demands:

Before I started meditating life was a grim ultra-marathon – especially looking after a child with a life-threatening condition who needs 24/7 care. I felt responsible for everything. It got done, but I was exhausted and had no time for myself and I was living on coffee, alcohol and adrenaline. Once I started meditating, each day became a relay. Twice a day, for twenty minutes I handed the baton over and recharged for the next leg and life felt sustainable again. Life has evolved so I go more with the flow and the day unfolds in the best possible way. The demands are as great as ever, but each day is better than I could have planned or imagined. Without any effort I have stopped drinking alcohol or coffee. It does feel miraculous, and the lives of everyone in the family are better for it. I don't have time not to meditate now.

Two ways to engage with change in your life

How do you feel when you experience big changes in your life?

At times, going through a transition may feel smooth and graceful. At other times it seems more rough and difficult. It helps to understand the two ways change tends to play out in our lives.

The first mode is *prospective change*. When change is prospective, you're on the front foot, moving with the evolutionary flow of life. The second is *reactive change*. This is when you're consciously (or unconsciously) going against the natural flow of life.

Let's line these two up against each other:

Prospective mode	Reactive mode
feels smooth, frictionless	feels rough, bumpy
respond quickly	react slowly
leaping into the unknown	waiting for it to be 'just right'
no overthinking	trying to figure it all out
no suffering	suffering
feeling clear, resolute	indecision, hesitation abound
a sense of enthusiasm	fearful, anxious
tuned in to direction of change	caught off guard, surprised

Prospective change happens when you see the direction nature is going and move fearlessly in that direction. Reactive change happens when you miss the cues that nature is giving you, and end up moving the wrong way. The more you tune in to what nature is up to, the smoother change will be.

Meditation helps you move onto the front foot by purifying and normalising your system. As a result, you're calmer and more perceptive. This refinement means you're able to detect what's going on in the subtler signals of life and move forward with more confidence and clarity.

Meditation makes you dynamic not manic

Sometimes I'm asked how meditation affects ambition levels and motivation. The concern people are voicing here is that meditation might make you so relaxed you lose the drive to succeed and achieve your goals. As one person said to me: 'I don't want to become too chilled out!' While they were interested in meditation as a tool to help them deal with stress and stay at the top of their game, they were also worried they might lose their edge.

Meditation doesn't turn you into some zoned-out bliss bunny. Quite the opposite. Inner peace is not about withdrawal from life. When you have more stability and awareness, you're more capable of dynamic, meaningful action.

Rather than making decisions from a place of stress-induced overexcitation, you have greater capacity to see the big picture. Your brain functioning is optimised. You're using more of the executive processing centre, rather than being driven by the limbic system, which shuts down thinking. With more energy and staying power you can up-level your functioning while staying calm and strategic.

Better health

Better health

When I speak about better health, I mean the health of the entire organism.

It used to be thought that if something was off in the body, it was a body functioning problem and, as with a machine, we needed to fix it. Now more and more medical experts recognise that separating mind and body makes no sense. Whatever's happening in the body is linked to what's happening at a deeper level.

As we've analysed, there's another aspect to be considered – consciousness. Everything in the universe is a manifestation of energy, including you. To truly understand this, we need to be regularly experiencing this most fundamental level of life, from which everything is being created.

Go to the source of the issue

As any good gardener will tell you, the most powerful way to tend to a plant and keep it healthy is to provide nourishment at its source. If a tree shows signs of being unwell, the wise gardener isn't only going to tend to the brittle branches, withering leaves and dried-up fruit. She'll also be working at the most basic level, watering and feeding the roots. Then nourishment can be drawn from the soil, which holds all the intelligence, bringing life and health back to the whole tree.

It's the same for you. When your mind and body are showing signs of being unwell, you'll get the most impact by going to the source of the issue and bringing nourishment to the deepest level. Rather than Band-Aid solutions that simply deal with the surface symptoms, you need to get to the underlying cause, in order to stay well and in balance.

What is that deepest level?

Back to tending to our tree. The outer layers of the tree consist of the very visible bark, branches, shiny green leaves and flowers. The inner layers are made up of a vast root system, hidden beneath the surface and less obvious. The clear, crystalline sap provides nourishment that permeates and gives life to every other aspect of the plant – unseen and at the basis of the whole organism.

The sap of the tree has everything that's needed to make branches and green leaves. It has everything that's needed to make flowers and fruit. On its own, it is non-fragrant, shapeless, formless and colourless. However, the sap has everything in it to make every product of the tree. So the colourless sap is the *un-manifest* totality of the entire plant.

Our life can also be viewed in a similar way:

1. The more expressed, outer layer of the **body**.
2. The more subtle, inner layer of the **mind**.
3. The underlying, invisible layer of **pure consciousness** or Being, that nourishes and permeates all aspects of the mind and body.

In this way, the 'colourless sap' of human life is consciousness. In its pure state, it's the source of mental energy in your mind. It's the underlying basis of every aspect of your physiology. Most importantly, it's the source of the healing intelligence of your whole system. When that intelligence is able to flow freely through the mind and all parts of the body, health will be maintained.

Consciousness conceives the body.
Consciousness constructs the body.

101

Consciousness governs the body.
Consciousness becomes the body.

Resilience is key

Illness is a result of disorder. Good health comes about by maintaining order. There's an interesting correlate in physics called the Meissner effect:

Internally coherent systems repel external, disruptive influences, while incoherent systems are easily penetrated by disorder from outside.

Another way to say this is that when a system is not orderly, it is weaker, less resilient and more susceptible to illness. To whatever extent you can maintain balance, this will be reflected in your ability to remain free from illness and premature ageing. You'll be stronger and healthier when your mind and body are coordinated and free from obstructions.

What is the root cause of most illness?

One word: *stress*. Of course factors such as hereditary conditions, body type, smoking, diet, pollution, work and sedentary lifestyles are all factors in illness. However, the research is clear – stress plays a major role.

Hans Selye wrote, 'Stress plays some role in the development of every disease'. And today the medical community recognises the vast majority of disease has its basis in the accumulation of emotional and physical stress. Some studies suggest up to 90 per cent of visits to the doctor have their origins in stress.

Stress disrupts the flow of intelligence in your physiology, manifesting as structural or functional abnormalities in your system.

These distortions eventually result in disease. The more stressed someone becomes, the weaker and less balanced their body will be. With continued overloads of experience the body becomes even weaker, less stable and more vulnerable. This is a downward spiral and at some point something will give.

Stress is the silent killer

Stress is often referred to as 'the silent killer' because it's not always easy to connect the dots and see how an illness can be traced back to stress. Sometimes though we can see it afterwards.

One of my students is a very successful businesswoman who does everything to the highest standards. She had worked for years as co-founder of a highly regarded media company. The business was expanding and had a roster of A-list clients. However, behind the scenes, things were not rosy. Her business partner was behaving unethically. His behaviour got worse over time and was having a direct and negative effect on my student. It all unravelled in a messy and acrimonious legal fight. And then she was diagnosed with cancer. Thankfully she caught it early and is now in excellent health. When we talked about what had happened, she directly linked that toxic situation with the reaction in her body. She'd been accumulating high levels of stress for years and it became too much.

As Dr Gabor Maté, an expert on stress and health, explains in his book *When the Body Says No*, 'Stress occurs when the demands made on an organism exceed that organism's reasonable capacities to fulfil them.'

Sometimes with disease we can trace it back to a specific situation that caused an increase in stress levels. But more often it's due to chronic stress that builds up over time. The legacy of old, accumulated stress will eventually be revealed. Like steam in a pressure cooker, it finds a way out.

The path from stress to disease

As we've seen, the sympathetic nervous system is one way the body deals with stress. Selye highlighted the importance of another central, focal point that is implicated in many diseases. It's known as the *hypothalamic-pituitary-adrenal axis* (or HPA axis) and is a major pivot point for how the mind connects to the body to deal with stress.

The hypothalamus is a brain region at the base of the skull connected to the pituitary gland. When you get stressed the hypothalamus is activated to produce a substance that stimulates the pituitary gland to produce the hormone *adrenocorticotrophic hormone* (ACTH). ACTH is carried by the blood to the adrenals. This leads to the secretion of stress neurochemicals called corticoids, the most common of which is cortisol.

As we've seen, the body is not designed to handle the continual release of stress hormones. Over time cortisol impacts nearly every part of the body, with particularly negative effects in a number of critical areas:

- Hormonal balance is disrupted, affecting many organs and tissues, including damage to blood vessels and the heart.
- Immune system functioning is compromised, limiting the body's ability to destroy infected or cancerous cells.
- Digestive system performance is inhibited, leading to inflammation and ulcers in the stomach and intestines.
- Blood sugar fluctuates due to elevated insulin release, leading to increased appetite, weight gain (particularly in the abdominal area), emotional imbalances and diabetes.

- Bone density is impaired by blocking calcium absorption, which decreases bone cell growth and increases the risk of osteoporosis.

The healing power of deep rest

Any time you're unwell the first instruction from your doctor is 'Get more rest.' Everywhere in nature we can see the regenerating effect of alternating rest with activity. Nature sleeps in the winter and bursts into action in the spring. The busyness of the day is preceded by the rest of the night. Regeneration is intrinsic to living – relax-and-renew is the direct opposite of fight-or-flight.

Rest is the counterbalance to the overexcitation of stress. Remember, we get stressed when we have an experience that our mind and body can't comfortably handle. Those experiences might be relatively simple or they might be more extreme. The load that is placed on the body and nervous system as a result of the experience leaves a deep impression on us. Sanskrit has a name for these impressions: *sanskaras*. Interestingly, this is where we get the English word scar. It's as if the impression has been etched into our mind and body.

The good news is that, with deep rest, these distortions are able to be dissolved and healed. This is where meditation makes the difference. Just as the mind can damage, the mind can also heal. By quieting the mind, the body self-repairs.

Research shows that some of the physical health conditions improved by automatic self-transcending meditation are:

- Heart disease
- Asthma

- High cholesterol
- High blood pressure
- Diabetes
- Cancer
- Digestive problems

My student Vivian talks about how she was able to come off her blood pressure medication:

> I always remember at the introductory talk you gave an example of a woman coming off her hypertension medication after learning to meditate. I thought bla bla bla... Well, it happened to me too. I took hypertensive drugs for seven years. I now no longer need medication. There are occasions that my blood pressure goes up, but I can control it via diet, breathing and meditation. It is incredible! I no longer have headaches, I make better diet choices, I have lots of energy and I sleep a lot less. I also quit smoking!

Another student shares how meditation supported her through her cancer treatments and beyond:

> I started meditation during my battle with cancer. At that time I was struggling with the side effects of chemotherapy and radiotherapy, heavy tiredness and insomnia. Meditating helped me recover physical strength. It also gave me the extra energy to get through the days of treatment. It helped physically and also mentally to be less anxious in the hospital. The hardest time for me was once treatments ended, as I was worried about the future and how to go back to a new normal. Meditating twice a day made me more grounded and free from overthinking. It became 'me time' that I feel is very precious.

Prevention must be the future of healthcare

There have been some outstanding breakthroughs in allopathic medicine that save and extend lives. But it's a system that relies on catching things at a very late stage. By the time someone is experiencing uncomfortable pressure in their chest, pain in their arms and shortness of breath, they're well down the path of serious imbalance in their system. At that late stage of cardiac arrest, the surgeon is playing catch-up and significant damage and distress is occurring.

Modern treatment relies heavily on medication to attempt to counteract an imbalance and compensate for deficiency. These synthetic medicines are never without side effects, sometimes more damaging over time than the issue they were trying to alleviate. Often they provide limited positive improvements that are not worth the mental and physical costs. Antibiotics are being prescribed so often, viruses and bacteria are increasingly mutating and becoming more resistant – very often within hospitals.

Huge amounts of money have been spent on research on the two big killers, heart disease and cancer. Yet they're still the most likely causes of death in the world. And with an ageing population, the spiralling costs of medical care are unsustainable.

The current approach isn't working. The future of healthcare needs to move away from an overly medicated, invasive and reactive system to one that is holistic, truly healing and able to address the root cause of disease. This requires an understanding of how consciousness is fundamental to the process. It's why practices like meditation have such value in bringing about a state of true balance and order.

a word about:

Meditation and Fertility

I work with a lot of couples who are having challenges conceiving. I know first-hand how tough this can be – the emotional highs and lows can be all-consuming and exhausting. There's no specific study that I'm aware of on how meditation affects fertility. However, we do know that stress is one of the major blocks to conceiving naturally. Once all the medical checks have been done and any complications are ruled out, the first thing to consider is how are your stress levels? As we've seen, when your body continually thinks it's running away from a predator, natural functions like menstruating, ovulating and reproducing humans get put to the bottom of the priority list.

When I first met Danusia she was in a lot of pain, physically and emotionally. She'd been trying to conceive for many years and had undergone multiple rounds of IVF. She was feeling increasingly desperate:

> I learned meditation when I hit rock bottom on my fertility journey – it came at a time when I needed it most. For the following four years, as I navigated this tough journey, I relied on my twice-daily meditation to help me through the emotional rollercoaster. I quickly became more calm, resilient, and accepting. This was noticed by family and friends, and many of them took up meditation as well. Meditation has continued to serve me well from pregnancy into motherhood, particularly boosting my energy levels.

Michelle talks about how learning to meditate brought her monthly cycle back into harmony:

I'm forty-seven and around the time I was thinking of learning to meditate, I started to miss my period for the first time in my life. Even though it seemed a bit early, I figured perhaps it was perimenopause. While I had missed three cycles at the time, it was not the main factor in my decision to learn, but rather seemed like it could be an added benefit. Within three weeks of meditating, my period came back and has been normal ever since.

Sustainable
happiness

Sustainable happiness

Life naturally evolves in the direction of happiness. We must constantly ask ourselves if what are we are doing is going to make us, and those around us, happy. Because happiness is the ultimate goal. It is the goal of all other goals.

Deepak Chopra, *Creating Affluence*

Expansion of happiness is the goal of human experience. We all want to be happy and fulfilled. It's a natural, deeply held impulse that drives all behaviour. And yet, you don't have to look far to see vast numbers of people are not feeling that way.

If happiness is what we're searching for, where is it?

Where are you looking to source your happiness? Is your happiness dependent upon others? Is it conditional upon circumstances being a certain way? Does your happiness rely upon the opinions of others? Is your state of fulfilment contingent upon events playing out according to a particular timetable and agenda?

In our highly competitive, individualistic and consumption-based society, this methodology for happiness is the norm. We're living in an age of **happiness via acquisition**.

Attempting to get happy through acquisition looks like this:

When I get that toy I'll be happy.
When I get the new bicycle I'll be happy.
When I pass those exams I'll be happy.
When I get that cute person to hang out with I'll be happy.
When I get that well paid job I'll be happy.

When I go on holiday to that sunny place I'll be happy.
When I buy that perfect house I'll be happy.
When I get that promotion I'll be happy.
When I have lots of zeros in my savings account I'll be happy.
When I retire with a chunky pension I'll be happy.

And so it goes on…

Operating from this model means life revolves around a never-ending jostle to acquire more. It's exhausting and futile. You get the new car. Then you want the bigger model. Then you want the faster, more efficient version. And then you want to go electric. And still you're not fulfilled. The innate desire for happiness is never satiated, because it's never enough and it's never permanent.

The fundamental mistake is the idea that things, people, circumstances and experiences will bring you *sustainable* happiness.

I'm not saying having lovely things, hanging out with wonderful people and enjoying amazing experiences are not worthwhile. Of course, these are all desirable and they bring *moments* of pleasure. However, those moments pass, because no thing, person or experience can provide you with lasting fulfilment. By their very nature, they are constantly changing. Therefore, counting on them to deliver a baseline of non-changing happiness won't work.

If it's not out there, then where is it?

It's inside you.

Lasting, stable fulfilment is found in a place that is lasting and stable. Beyond the ever-changing, relative layers. Beyond space and time. Beyond boundaries. Transcendent, pure bliss.

Waves on an ocean rise and fall. And the ocean remains. Like a wave on an ocean, you're not separate from the world around you. You are the wave and the ocean simultaneously. Just as the baseline of every wave is the ocean beneath it, pure consciousness or Being is your ground state.

Meditation is the technique to settle down your individual 'wave' on that ocean of consciousness.

From our very first meditation our thinking settles down and we begin to experience the ocean of pure consciousness deep inside. We do this every day, and we identify more and more with this grounded inner aspect of non-changing bliss and energy. Rather than feeling lonely and small, we move to a sense of feeling connected and big.

As we capture that oceanic status, our identity transforms from a feeling of dislocation and separation to one of being grounded and interconnected. When this most fundamental relationship is established, when small self knows big Self, then we are becoming free of fear. We know who we are. We're no longer reliant upon the ever-changing world to deliver our fulfilment. And our sense of confidence in our own life and destiny is transformed.

To whatever degree you have access to stable, inner fulfilment, then to that degree you'll experience peace and happiness in your life.

Meditation develops a self-referral state

At your source you are the creative energy from which everything in the universe is manifesting. This is your big Self – your universal aspect. That part of you that connects to the Absolute, unified aspect of nature, a field of non-change that is the basis of all life in the universe. Your small self is your individual aspect – your individual likes and dislikes, your personality, characteristics and traits, your unique mind–body make-up.

Contact with your big Self is a *self-referral* experience. A process of Self-Realisation. Realisation of your true Self. When your reference point is your spirit rather than the objects of experience, you are in a state of self-referral.

When your reference point is the ever-changing relative world, you are *object-referral*. In that state, your identity and your happiness relies upon people, things, events and circumstances. Your sense of stability relies on those aspects of life not changing. Often this leads to controlling behaviour because you need things to stay a certain way to feel stable and happy. It's a fragile state, because people and circumstances constantly change. We're like a ship unmoored – buffeted about by the ever-changing world. We only feel okay as long as we have the power that comes from acquiring money, status, experiences and stuff. Take those things away, and our identity crumbles.

A life lived in object-referral is essentially a life lived in a state of fear. Fear of missing out. Fear of others getting more than me. Fear of not being good enough. Fear of things changing. And fear is the opposite of happiness.

Locus of control

A parallel concept is a psychological measure known as *locus of control*. This reflects the degree to which a person believes they have responsibility for their life versus the degree to which external forces are driving their experience. When your locus of control is based on external circumstances, chance events, the opinions of others and the pressures of society, you feel like a victim of situations that are beyond your control. Studies show that a strong external locus of control correlates with more stress and depression.

Contrast this with someone whose locus of control is more on the internal end of the continuum. They are more likely to make a direct connection between their own actions and what happens in their life. They recognise their actions have consequences. This is empowering. Stationed in a stable sense of Self, you feel grounded, more fulfilled and less shaken by changes around you.

An example of greater internal locus of control is beautifully expressed by Lily, who learned to meditate when she was twelve years old:

I came to meditation as a child because my mother was a meditator. As a working mum with a demanding career, she would arrive home often frazzled or jet-lagged. After a quick hello, she'd make a beeline for the sofa, shut her eyes for twenty minutes, and emerge refreshed and grounded. I was curious to experience this for myself, and so Jillian taught me to meditate shortly before my thirteenth birthday.

I noticed benefits immediately, even as a child with little to worry about beyond submitting my homework on time. The world looked a little sharper, as if in high definition. I needed less sleep than my friends, was less prone to conflict and, in the playground, had an intuitive sense of which kids to stay away from. When I was nervous, I was still able to think clearly in exams and speak fluidly in interviews. I don't think meditation gave me any superpowers in this respect – it simply ensured I was never incapacitated by nerves, stress or fatigue. It definitely helped me to reach my full potential academically.

This is not to say that life was breezy from the age of twelve onwards. Like most teenagers I partied hard and was prone to peer pressure and often hard on myself. There were plenty of meltdowns and tearful calls home. But I always recovered from these moments quickly, as if moored to a steadfast place of peace and self-assurance. Throughout the inevitable ups and downs of adolescence, meditation offered a reliable and portable practice to return to whenever I felt adrift.

Meditation had other effects, which, though I was slightly embarrassed at the time, I'm grateful for now. For example, I was acutely sensitive to the smell of cigarette smoke and found nightclubs deafeningly loud. Similarly, I could not understand the allure of recreational drugs. Why bother, when I could already access a safe, natural and free 'high' twice a day? Friends would roll their eyes and tease me for behaving as if my 'body was a temple'. Several of the same friends have since learned to meditate, reporting the same heightening of their senses and a diminished interest in alcohol.

Having learned to meditate at a young age, I used to worry that I could not distinguish between my 'inherent self' and the long-term effects of meditation. I now realise those two things aren't separate. Growing up is hard, and meditation helped me to navigate the process as smoothly and happily as possible. I feel truly blessed to have become a meditator at an early age, and only wish more children could have the same experience.

Contact with bliss is blissful

As we've seen, by orienting the mind towards progressively greater happiness, the mind reaches a point of deep inner peace. One of the characteristics of the inner state of Being is bliss. Contact with that state of bliss is blissful. What you see, you become. When you realise that unbounded inner state and are able to experience it more and more, you stabilise those qualities of blissfulness, energy and perfect balance. With that inner baseline as your reference point, you're not constantly seeking happiness in places that cannot deliver.

Meditation activates the neurochemistry of happiness

Let's bring this back to a more tangible and measurable level. Science shows that there's a very particular cocktail of neuro-hormones associated with happiness, which are the opposite of the biochemistry of stress. This endogenous cocktail of bliss chemistry is activated when people meditate. Meditators are not simply making a mood of feeling good: 'Hey man, I'm a meditator, everything's cool.' We can actually measure a difference in their biochemistry when they settle down and move away from a heightened state.

Neurotransmitters are often referred to as the body's chemical messengers. They are chemical substances used by the nervous system to transmit messages between neurons, by bridging the tiny gap (synapse) that separates nerve cells. Imbalances in the brain's neurotransmitters are linked to a number of mental and physical diseases.

Meditation boosts serotonin – the happy chemical

One such chemical messenger is serotonin. Low levels of serotonin are linked to feeling sad, depressed, suicidal and aggressive. This is reflected in the massive upsurge in prescriptions for *selective serotonin reuptake inhibitors* (SSRIs). SSRIs are a class of drugs that are typically used as antidepressants in the treatment of depression and anxiety. They work by binding with a receptor in brain cells that increases the output of serotonin. In England, the number of antidepressants dispensed has doubled in the last decade and the same trend is playing out in the US, with a 64 per cent increase in use over a five-year period. Women are twice as likely than men to be prescribed antidepressants.

Research shows those who meditate have a higher baseline level of serotonin, correlating positively with more upbeat emotions, satisfaction and blissfulness. These levels are naturally occurring without the unwanted side effects of SSRIs.

Meditation deactivates the neurochemistry of fear

All fear is based in lack of knowledge of what's going on, what's likely to be going on and what has gone on in the past. If you have enough knowledge about anything you can't be frightened. This is why we don't let little children watch scary movies. They lack the understanding that comes from a broader context in which to interpret things. They don't have as much awareness as adults. Yet even as adults, our brains are capable of much more awareness.

The biochemistry of fear is the opposite of the biochemistry of happiness. It's natural to have moments of nervous tension or anxiety before a big event like sitting an important exam or giving a presentation to a room full of people. However, when the anxiety remains in your system even though the demanding situation has passed, it becomes an issue. This is called trait anxiety, and it has negative effects on sleep, energy and feelings of happiness and well-being. A meta-analysis comparing a range of techniques found that automatic self-transcending meditation had more than twice the effect on reducing trait anxiety compared to other meditation and relaxation techniques. Interestingly, practising a concentration-based meditation was shown to be worse than doing nothing, indicating that controlling and focusing the mind can actually raise anxiety levels.

Panic attacks and the acidity connection

It has long been known that blood-lactate levels are linked with anxiety and stress. In 1969, a study published in *Scientific American* titled 'The Biochemistry of Anxiety' showed that patients with anxiety neurosis or panic disorder had an excessive amount of lactic acid in their blood. When someone is having a panic attack they experience an intense fear of impending doom without any apparent cause. The effects are debilitating and the fatigue that results is intense.

As discussed earlier, the amygdala in the brain plays a crucial role in activating the fear response when you perceive a threat. One by-product of this is increased adrenaline levels, and this creates excess lactate production. A more recent study in the same journal observed changes in the brain linked to recurring panic attacks. The results showed that acidity in the brain plays an essential role in fear, indicating that patients with panic disorder tend to generate excess lactic acid in their brains.

There are many studies demonstrating that lactic acid levels reduce in meditators. This tendency towards a more alkaline biochemistry points to a relaxed, happy and stress-free state.

Annie learned to meditate shortly after giving birth and shares how her panic attacks stopped with meditation:

> When I learned to meditate I was struggling with post-natal anxiety, wasn't sleeping and felt like my mind had turned against me. I was having panic attacks at night and felt like I was falling apart. Within ten days of starting to meditate I felt calmer and was sleeping

better. I grew more accepting of the anxiety I was feeling and learned how to sit with emotions and not judge them. Within three months the panic attacks had stopped, I was sleeping through the night, I changed my diet and was engaging with the world again.

Meditation and medication

If someone is taking medication for anxiety or depression, it's not a barrier to learning to meditate. Very often, students will come to meditation with a desire to come off their medication. Over time, with regular meditation, this is generally the trend. However, this should always be done carefully in consultation with your GP.

Here's the experience of one of our students who came off her medication gradually, after a few years of meditating each day:

I came to meditation with a history of depression and anxiety that had begun in my teens, and followed me into my mid-twenties. I would go up and down in cycles, and thought it was just something that I had to deal with. I went on and off antidepressants and went through a couple of major breakdowns, which were completely debilitating. I was perpetually in fear of not knowing where my life was going. I thought I would never 'find' happiness.

Then I learned to meditate, and truly everything changed. I started experiencing a deep sense of knowing that everything would be okay – in fact, better than just okay. I became comfortable with myself. I learned to listen to my inner voice, that knew which direction to take me in, rather than resist and ignore my feelings because they were uncomfortable, or went against the flow of what I thought I should be doing. I am now a calm, resilient, joyful person, excited about the future, with a zest for life that I never imagined I would or could have. With the backbone of my meditation practice bringing me stability and a deep sense of knowingness, I came off my antidepressants for good. The experience was smooth and surprisingly beautiful – I realised I had been numbing my ability to feel, because I'd been afraid to feel anything too intensely. Now, I feel the full spectrum of emotions from a place of understanding, rather than fear. Even in the most intense moments of sadness or pain, I know these will pass. I have a much healthier relationship with my body, my intuition, and my mind. This isn't overstating it – meditation saved my life.

a word about:

Meditation and Addiction

We're all dependent on something. I'm dependent on fresh air, food, water, human contact and rest. These are what I call 'good dependencies'. By having more of them, I'm enriched, sustained and nourished. And then there are the 'not-so-good dependencies' – those things that, when you have more and more of them, have a detrimental impact, mentally, physically or socially.

When someone feels anxious, bored, lacking self-worth or without purpose, it's natural to seek escape. This might be in the form of buying a new outfit or going on a sunny holiday to bring about a temporary uplift in mood. Another way to fill the void is to turn to drugs – prescribed or recreational. However, *the reliance on drugs to provide a heightened, more pleasurable experience of life is grounded on the false premise that something out there will make us feel better. As we've seen, the search for fulfilment is a natural and honourable one. However, to continually seek fulfilment in places where it doesn't exist leads to misery.*

This is where meditation reorients the seeker. By diving in and locating stable, non-changing fulfilment inside, the need for external substances or experiences goes down. The research consistently demonstrates this. Use of tobacco, alcohol and illicit drugs tend to fall away for meditators, and more quickly than with standard substance abuse programmes. Whereas conventional programmes tend to have high levels of relapse within a few months, abstinence rates in meditators last longer. My experience is that the longer someone is meditating, the more likely it is they will stop, or significantly reduce, their consumption of drugs.

Here's what Marc has to say about how meditation has been crucial on his path to recovery:

Meditation is one of the key tools in my recovery and spiritual programme. Learning to meditate was a milestone in my life, helping me discover self-awareness and connection. I describe it as seeing the world with my eyes open. In fact all my senses seem to work with more clarity – I now see and hear more of what's going on around me.

For me, meditation is a daily journey not a destination. Continually refreshing my mind and body to deal with the day's challenges as well as allowing some of the old buried stuff to surface. Meditation enables me to feel clear, it declutters my mind so I can make decisions from a place of calm.

Acceptance, clarity, connection, self-awareness... some of the positive effects meditation has had. Meditation guides me towards letting go, surrender, and not wanting to control – the same characteristics that are so important in my 12-Step programme. Day by day I choose to follow a spiritual pathway, day by day I choose to meditate – the two are interwoven.

Clearer thinking

Clearer thinking

When people come along to learn to meditate we ask them what they want to get out of it. Time and again people identify mental functioning as one of the main areas they're looking to upgrade.

'I want to be more focused in my thinking.'
'I want more mental clarity.'
'I want to improve my concentration.'
'I want my mind to be less scattered.'

The 10 per cent claim

It's often stated that human beings only use a fraction of their brain. Often the claim is we're only using around 10 per cent. It's unclear exactly where this number originated; however, modern imaging techniques don't support it anyway. There is a significant degree of engagement in the brain even when a very simple task is being performed. *Functional magnetic resonance imaging* (fMRI) scans shows even the simple act of clenching both hands engages a lot more than a tenth of your brain.

Nonetheless, people still do feel like they're not performing to the degree that they could. So where does this leave us?

The idea that we can improve our performance by accessing more of the brain's potential is certainly a powerful one. However, I believe we need to be asking the question slightly differently. Instead of looking at the *quantity* of engagement we need to shift to the *quality* of engagement.

The real question to ask is:

Are we optimising the full potential of our vast and sophisticated nervous system?

The American psychologist and philosopher William James inferred this in his book, *The Energies of Men*. All the way back in 1908 he wrote that as a species we 'are making use of only a small part of our possible mental and physical resources.'

The brain is by far the most complex organ in the human body. Tens of billions of neurons interact in a vast and intricate web of interconnectivity.

Weighing on average about three pounds, the human brain has a staggering range of potential capabilities. The electrophysiological and biochemical functions that are involved in you reading this sentence are immense, let alone what's involved as you drive your car, listen to a podcast, while at the same time talking to your mother about someone you met two weeks ago. Human brains are relatively large, in particular the frontal cortex, which is viewed as key to the capacity for higher human functioning. We have an advanced ability for using language, adapting the environment to our needs and learning from past experiences. We're able to demonstrate self-awareness – awareness of our thoughts and actions – and then modify our behaviour and decisions based upon that observation.

The brain takes much longer to reach full development than any other organ and it develops in a different way. Most organs develop their basic structure while in the womb, and then grow in size through cellular division. The opposite happens with the brain. A toddler will have their full complement of about 100 billion neurons by about two years old. However, the structural development continues over time, as the nerve cells form trillions of intricate connections.

Over the course of your life you'll lose about one billion neurons, but this loss is compensated for by the number of connections between cells increasing. This happens via the filaments that extend out of each cell in a branch-like pattern. These fibres are called dendrites (from the Greek word *dendron*, which means 'tree'). Dendrites receive electrical impulses and are crucial connectors between cells. Experiments show it's possible for cells to open up new channels of communication by growing new dendrites.

There's a misconception that brain functioning automatically begins to deteriorate from early adulthood – most likely linked to the fact that neurons begin to die from that point onwards. However, longitudinal studies show that in healthy brains there is no reduction in IQ into old age. And there are plenty of examples of individuals with thriving, alert minds well into later life. Higher brain functioning can be sustained, and even expanded, over time.

Our brains are constantly changing

Your brain structure evolves over time. Rather than being static, the brain is highly dynamic. It's constantly reorganising and building itself in response to internal and external experiences. This phenomenon of changeability is called *neuroplasticity*.

According to the Oxford Dictionary, neuroplasticity is:

The ability of the brain to form and reorganise synaptic connections, especially in response to learning or experience or following injury.

Neuroplasticity is the change in neural pathways and synapses (the tiny connections between neurons) that occur due to behaviour, environment or neural processes. During such changes, the brain engages in synaptic pruning, deleting the neural connections that are no longer necessary or useful, and strengthening the ones that are needed. Your brain is *constantly* creating and losing connections. It's estimated that about 70 per cent of synaptic connections change each day!

This process of transformation is most active in childhood. A child has double the number of brain connections of an adult. It's this high level of brain connections from ages three to ten that allows us to learn language, rule-governed behaviour and socialisation. At around ten years old a child begins to prune connections between brain cells. Brain connections that have been used remain. Connections that have not been used drop off.

Form adapts to function – what you do with your brain changes it

Our brains are constantly being shaped by experience – both positive and negative. Everything you learn, every action you take and everything you perceive, changes your brain. And we know this process starts early when the growing foetus is in the womb.

The richness and variety of the environment in a child's very early years has been shown to have a huge impact on their mental development. Many studies have shown that early life experiences can influence brain development in children.

One fascinating example is Edith Stern, whose father Aaron was a survivor of Nazi concentration camps. In the 1950s he decided he would give his newborn daughter an incredibly rich and varied environment from the time she was born. Classical music played in the home. He talked to her as much as possible and baby talk was forbidden. By four and a half she'd read *Encyclopaedia Britannica, Volume 1*. By age six, she was reading the *New York Times* and at least two books every day. Her IQ score was at 'genius' levels and she graduated from university at the age of fifteen. This is an extreme example to make a point. While her education was intensively intellectual and lacked an all-round approach, it shows an amazing level of development that's possible when a child is exposed to high levels of stimulation and encouragement early on.

Give your brain a boost with music

Playing a musical instrument is an activity that's shown to enhance and build neural connections within the brain. Learning to play music in childhood provides many benefits that can last a lifetime and help compensate for diminished performance later in life. Those many hours spent learning and practising specific types of motor control and coordination seem to provide an added defence against memory loss and cognitive decline in old age.

Learn another language and grow your hippocampus

Learning a foreign language has also been shown to change the brain. Swedish scientists used brain scans to monitor what happens when someone learns a second language. Young adult military recruits with a flair for languages learned Arabic, Russian or Dari intensively. A control group of medical students also studied hard, but not at languages. MRI scans showed specific parts of the brains of the language students developed in size, whereas the brain structures of the control group remained unchanged. The parts that developed in size were the hippocampus, a deep-lying brain structure that's involved in learning new material and spatial navigation, as well as three areas in the cerebral cortex.

London cab drivers have bigger brains

In order to drive a traditional black cab in London, drivers must learn 'The Knowledge' – a thorough understanding of the myriad of streets within a six-mile radius of Charing Cross. It takes around three years of hard training, and 75 per cent of those who embark on the course drop out along the way. Research by scientists at University College showed that London taxi drivers who were given MRI brain scans had a larger hippocampus compared with other people. The scientists also found the posterior hippocampus was more developed in taxi drivers who had been in the career for forty years than in those who had been driving for a shorter period. So if you want to improve your memory, turn off your GPS and learn to navigate around town!

How stress affects the brain

On a less positive note, when you're experiencing high levels of stress and fatigue, different parts of the brain are engaged. A phenomenon known as 'downshifting' occurs, as the frontal, thinking part of the brain shuts down and the rear, more primitive part of the brain is activated. The prefrontal cortex is often referred to as the 'CEO of the brain', because it represents the higher human, executive processing centre. It connects to all other parts of the brain, and takes input from the rear, sensory part of the brain in order to drive decision-making, organisation and planning.

When you're in flight-or-flight mode, the prefrontal cortex goes offline and the focus shifts to the immediate, concrete present. As the amygdala takes over, broader perspective is lost and you move to reaction mode, responding to the stimuli that are right in front of you. You lose the more integrated functioning of the front part of the brain. This directly limits the repertoire of behaviours and creative solutions you can come up with in that moment. Rather than making connections and seeing possible underlying causes, everything narrows down.

What we see in people who are under stress over a long period of time is that the front part of the brain shrinks in size. Likewise, the hippocampus, which has to do with memory, is also physically smaller in those who experience chronic stress. Fortunately, the brain's malleability becomes a positive when we care for it in the best way. Rather than accepting that mental faculties will automatically decline with age, we can unlock the tremendous potential of the brain by supporting it with the right experiences and nourishment, including meditation.

How we nourish our brain will impact its functioning

Nature knows – the brain is our most valuable organ and deserves protection above all else.

The impact of malnutrition on brain functioning is particularly important – so much so that we have an inbuilt protective mechanism called 'brain sparing'. If there's a lack of essential nourishment in the form of vitamins, amino acids and oxygen, then the organism makes sure other organs are deprived first. The brain gets top priority for as long as possible.

Although the brain is only about 3 per cent of the body's total weight, it consumes 20 per cent of its oxygen intake. Oxygen is essential to brain functioning. We know that when oxygen flow is disrupted, brain functioning is limited, and if the brain is starved of oxygen even for only a few minutes, irreparable damage occurs.

Every two seconds, someone in the world will have a stroke. The US Centers for Disease Control and Prevention state that about 87 per cent of all strokes in the US are due to blood flow to the brain being blocked due to a narrowing of the carotid arteries, the main arteries supplying the brain.

Again, to understand why this happens we come back to the negative effects of stress. As we've seen, when you get stressed, your heart rate speeds up, blood pressure rises, and the body goes into neurochemical overkill, with the release of stress hormones to mobilise the system. When the nervous system is chronically activated in this way, it damages the blood vessel walls, leading to their thickening, which is called arteriosclerosis.

We see a very different pattern with meditation. Studies indicate an *increase in cerebral blood flow* to both the front and back of the brain in meditators. This increased blood flow nourishes the brain with oxygen and nutrients, allowing for increased brain cell activity. A meditator reports this as feeling more alert and awake after meditation.

How meditation rewires your brain

The brain you have today will be very different to the brain you have tomorrow. This is incredibly empowering. Your experiences impact the functioning of your brain, and the quality of that functioning determines the quality of functioning of your mind. A calm and alert brain will lead to a calm and alert mind.

Because your brain is not 'hard-wired' like your laptop, you can forge new pathways and inter-neuronal connections, with repetition of any activity. Keep practising your backhand for six hours a day and new connections build in the muscles and the brain. Sit down to meditate each day and you rewire your brain in a coordinated and powerful way. Every meditation session is like pushing the reset button, affecting every aspect of your physical and mental functioning.

Brain-wave patterns with meditation

One of the most common ways to measure brain activity in meditation is with an electroencephalogram (EEG). It's a relatively easy, non-invasive way to measure minute electrical patterns on the surface of the brain. EEG patterns are broadly arranged according to the frequency (cycles per second) of the electrical wave as follows:

Type of wave	Frequency (Hz)	Condition when present
Gamma	20–50	awake, concentrating hard
Beta	18–30	awake, active, eyes open
Alpha	8–10	awake, relaxed, eyes closed
Theta	5–7	awake, in children
Delta	0.5–4	deep sleep

In an automatic self-transcending technique of meditation, we see an increase in alpha brain waves, associated with relaxation and a lack of anxiety. These reflect the state of restful alertness described earlier. The meditator is in a wakeful, hypo-metabolic state – deeply rested and yet alert at the same time.

Just as brain patterns vary in different states of consciousness, they are also different for different styles of meditation. Focused attention techniques, like metta meditation (loving-kindness and compassion), are characterised by beta/gamma activity. Open monitoring techniques like mindfulness are characterised by theta activity.

Increased activity in the prefrontal cortex

The prefrontal cortex is the highly complex, processing centre in your brain. It's involved in creative problem-solving, short-term memory, decision-making, planning, values, moral reasoning and sense of self. It's what contributes to our ability to think in an abstract and multilayered way. Neural imaging shows this frontal area is more active in automatic self-transcending meditation. This reflects the state of restful alertness that's activated – heightened alertness in the midst of deep silence for the mind and body. Given the capacity of the brain to change, over time the brain normalises this optimal functioning. Rather than solely noticing differences during meditation, changes begin to stabilise and become the new normal outside of meditation.

This upgrade quickly results in the following improvements to mental functioning:

- Improved short- and long-term memory
- More creative problem-solving
- Greater ability to concentrate and focus
- Critical thinking and enhanced learning ability
- Better decision-making

Here's Mark's report on how meditation has improved his mental functioning:

I feel more focused and have much more mental capacity to get things done. When I'm doing tasks I find I don't have as much 'A.D.D.' as I used to. Before I always felt like I was racing against the clock. Now I'm accomplishing more and I find myself with extra time in my day. I'm actively looking for ways to fill it!

And David, a 33-year-old banker, explains how his mental clarity changed very quickly:

> I can definitely attest to the benefits of meditation – and it's been less than a week. I'm more focused at work, less 'triggered' by incidental, unimportant happenings in the office. My thinking is clearer and more focused and I feel that I have more capacity to adapt to a fluid working environment. Out of the office I feel more centred and grounded – less manic and frazzled.

In addition to meditation rewiring and upgrading the physical brain circuitry, there's another important change that occurs. By removing the obstructing effect of stress, the senses are freed up to have clear and unimpeded access to the environment.

Reduce the noise-to-signal ratio

We all know the feeling when the mind is buzzy and full of thoughts; it's hard to work out what to do next. You can't think clearly because of the tsunami of thoughts that keep coming.

This is a function called the *noise-to-signal ratio*. Think of an old transistor radio that's full of static. It's impossible to get a clear signal and hear the news report because of the unwanted noise that's in the way. When your mind is jammed full of thoughts, it's like the old radio. The noise of the mental chatter drowns out any signal about what to do next. You can't get clear about what to say or do with all that obstruction in the way.

Meditation is one of the most powerful ways to shift the noise-to-signal ratio in your mind. Turn down the volume on the buzzy thoughts and you're able to get an unambiguous signal about what to do rather than being overwhelmed by the cacophony in your head.

My friend Debbie, a highly sought-after executive coach, recommends meditation to her clients for this very reason. Here's what she says about how important it is in order for her clients to be available for the work:

I need the individuals whom I support to be receptive, focused and reflective. If a person is in constant physical and cognitive motion, overexciting their body and mind, as well as not taking time to rest, it is a challenge for them to learn the necessary techniques to upgrade their communication.

A typical example is a project manager who came to me as a result of her boss giving some highly critical feedback about her communication style at work. She was seen as aggressive, strident and too forceful. Her way of working with people was causing conflict and distress.

My early sessions with her were long and intense; her way of speaking was fast with visible signs of physical and emotional overexcitement and stress. After a few sessions I realised that I could give her all the tools and techniques in my box, but without some fundamental change, we weren't going to achieve anything sustainable back in the workplace.

I helped her understand that she needed to take some time out and do some work on herself before we could continue. We built a plan to include meditation, yoga and some personal downtime.

To her credit she followed the plan and was able to reach a new level of consciousness, which impacted everything, including her communication and leadership style.

Occasionally I meet someone who has already worked this out. I coached a man who was in a new leadership role and needed help in developing a communication plan for his organisation. From our very first meeting I could sense a difference. He was focused, attentive, empathetic, decisive and clear about his goals. He was prepared to invest the time to learn new tools and techniques, to reflect on his team and their needs, as well as to ensure he had balance in his own life. After several meetings he mentioned to me that he had learned to meditate some years before, after experiencing a traumatic personal loss. He believed meditation had not only saved him from collapse himself, but also enabled him to support others in a much more effective way.

a word about:

The Importance of Water for the Brain

In her excellent book The XX Brain, *Dr Lisa Mosconi highlights the importance of staying hydrated in terms of optimal brain functioning. 'The brain itself is 80 per cent water. Every chemical reaction that takes place in the brain depends on water. The brain is so sensitive to dehydration that even a minimal lack of water can cause symptoms like brain fog, fatigue, dizziness, confusion, headache, and most alarmingly, brain shrinkage.'*

It might seem a very obvious point; however, our brains depend on optimal hydration to function well. Water is essential for increasing blood flow, oxygen and nutrients to the brain, while at the same time providing cushioning and lubrication to brain tissue. It's fascinating how many people report being thirsty when they first learn to meditate. After just a few meditations, their system quiets down and they get a true read on how dehydrated they are. I'm sure much of the population is chronically dehydrated and such a simple issue is having a huge impact on well-being, including mental functioning.

Hot Water

In Ayurveda, the ancient science of natural healthcare, how we consume water is as important as the quantity. On a recent trip to India I met a woman who prided herself on being very healthy. Despite drinking litres of water each day she complained, 'I can't drink enough and I'm always thirsty.' She'd noticed me sipping my mug of hot water and wanted to know why, in the scorching summer, I was filling my body with more heat!

As my Ayurvedic doctor explained, it's a question of absorption. Water that has been boiled before being drunk will be absorbed more quickly by the cells of the body than cold water. When this woman started sipping boiled water, her constant thirst disappeared.

Instruction: Sip boiled water every thirty minutes throughout the day. It's the regularity that's important. I tend to boil the kettle and fill my Thermos so I have it on my desk. I always start the day by sipping a cup of very warm boiled water. If you want to add a slice of lemon you can, although plain is best.

Three reasons to drink hot water:

1. More nourishment
   According to Ayurveda, we get maximum digestibility from our food by cooking it. When we 'cook' water by boiling it, it will be more effectively absorbed by the body and therefore more nourishing and balancing.
2. Peak purification
   Imagine a blocked drain, clogged up with gunk. Hot water is going to be more effective than cold water in clearing it out. In the same way, our body is made up of millions of super-fine channels ('shrotas' in Ayurveda) that over time accumulate toxins, fatty deposits and the residue of undigested food. The most effective way to clear this unwanted toxicity out of the body is to sip hot water and flush the system. The intelligence of the body then flows without obstruction.
3. Dependable digestion
   Digestion depends on our ability to burn up the food we consume. If our 'digestive fire' is burning strongly, we'll be able to convert food into energy without building up undigested residue that turns toxic and leads to disease. Drinking cold water is like dumping a load of iced water on a fire. The digestive flame goes out, and the food is unable to be processed, remaining in the body as toxins.

Enhanced creativity

Enhanced creativity

The story goes that Sir Isaac Newton, sitting under a tree, watched an apple drop to the ground. In that relaxed state, he was able to make an association between the apple falling and the moon orbiting the Earth, and so the theory of gravity came about.

We've all had moments when a spark of a good idea comes to us at the most unusual moment. I remember working with a guy who was a partner in a big management consultancy. His wife used to get frustrated with him standing in the shower for twenty minutes each morning, but his response was, 'That's when I get all my good ideas!' It's like when your friend asks you for the name of an actor in an old movie, and try as you might, you can't remember. Then three hours later, when you're cooking dinner, it pops into your mind.

Your best ideas don't come to you when you're worked up and straining. When you settle down, you're more able to slip into a state where you catch those nuggets of inspiration.

This is why meditation is a key tool for greater creativity. The mind de-excites to quieter layers of thinking, steps beyond the faintest impulse of thought, and experiences the source of creative energy and intelligence – pure awareness. And this is not an abstract speculation. As we discussed, science has identified this least-excited state. Having touched that state, the meditator then comes back into activity, infused with more energy, intelligence and clarity.

What does it mean to be creative?

Creativity has two aspects. It might be to produce something original, unique and not seen before. It might also involve taking existing knowledge, forms and phenomena and combining them in a new and innovative way. Creation often involves both of these approaches. When I speak about creativity I'm referring to it in the broadest sense. Rather than just being restricted to artistic pursuits or a particular profession, creativity can be seen in an elegantly produced spreadsheet, a nourishing meal or an engaging lesson plan for schoolchildren. Creativity is fundamental to the process of life – every thought and action has the potential to be creative.

Creativity involves both left and right hemispheres

Your brain is divided into left and right halves, which are connected by a massive bundle of nerves, the corpus callosum. The left side of the brain receives sensations from, and directs, the right side of the body and vice versa. So when you reach for someone's right hand, it's the left side of the brain that registers the touch and controls the movement.

The two hemispheres are not mirror images of each other and they perform very different functions. The left hemisphere controls verbal, logical and rational functions by processing the details of experience. The right hemisphere integrates the bigger context and supports image recognition, aesthetic appreciation, spatial relationships, music awareness and imagination.

These differences have given rise to the common misconception that if you're left-brain dominant you're going to be better at science and if you're right-brain dominant, you're more suited to the arts. This is not only a limited view of how we use our magnificent brains, it's also inaccurate.

Neural imaging studies indicate that *both* sides of the brain are engaged in creative acts. The more original, elaborate and complex the creative output, the higher the level of activity in the frontal areas of both sides of the brain. Anything that integrates and synthesises both hemispheres of the brain is going to generate an upsurge in creativity. The creative person is one who can think out of the box by making spontaneous cross-connections and then find a way to express that, verbally or visually.

Greater synchrony and brain coherence

In our society we tend to recognise and reward the more left-brain analytical functions. Schoolchildren generally spend far more time on reading, writing and arithmetic than they do on art and music. When I was at school, if we performed well on left-brain tasks, only then were we rewarded with some right-brain time for art and drawing as a 'treat'. However, our brains and our creativity can't be compartmentalised like this.

Split-brain research indicates that creativity is associated with the degree of *integration* of the cerebral hemispheres. This brain functioning can be seen in the so-called 'Aha moment' in the creative process when a sudden realisation occurs – just like Newton's insight about the falling apple. EEG studies show that the two brain hemispheres become more *coherent* in a similar way during automatic self-transcending meditation. This means brain-wave patterns become more orderly – the same pattern of brain waves appear in different regions of the brain. The various parts of the brain are talking to each other in a functional way.

As you read this, the brain waves in your two cerebral hemi-spheres are firing in different, seemingly unrelated ways. If you were to put the book down and start meditating, we'd see the brain waves start to fall into line with each other – evidence of synchrony between both sides. The EEG shows these peak moments happening many times throughout a meditation. Over time this optimised creative state becomes more stable outside of meditation, resulting in more good ideas and insights.

There's another type of orderliness that's seen in the brains of meditators, called *global coherence*. The whole brain is engaged as alpha brain waves spread from the back of the brain in a coherent way over the entire brain to the frontal region. This enhanced coordination between the sensory centres in the back and the motor controls in the front suggests a greater potential for integration of thought and action. Interestingly, we see an improvement in reaction times and mind–body coordination in meditators immediately after meditation and in ongoing activity.

Why more consciousness makes you more creative

Shortly after his enlightenment, the Buddha was approached by some men who recognised him to be a very extraordinary being. They asked him: 'Are you a god?' 'No,' he replied. 'Are you a reincarnation of God?' 'No,' he replied. 'Are you a wizard, then?' 'No.' 'Are you a man?' 'No.' 'What are you?' they asked. He replied, 'I am awake.'

In meditation we rest profoundly. As a result, we dissolve stress and tiredness faster than we gain it. We become more con-scious. More aware. *We wake up.* And it's this wakefulness that allows us to see the world with more clarity and lucidity.

The opposite happens the more stressed and excited we are. We're less perceptive and more likely to miss the cues and opportunities around us. We risk sailing into waters that we shouldn't be entering. Time gets wasted, and we pay the price for missing the signals of nature and fighting to correct mistakes. It's costly, because it robs us of the ability to station ourselves in creation mode.

There are three hallmarks of being more aware that fund your creative power:

1. You **access a broader spectrum of reality**. Just like a wide-angle lens on a camera, you can fit more things into your awareness at the same time. When you're tired and distracted, your awareness gets squeezed down and it's hard to hold more than one thing in your attention in any moment.
2. You gain greater **ability to detect subtlety**. Your capacity to see fine differences, and discriminate between things that seem very similar, goes up as wakefulness increases. This is the basis of intelligence – being able to evaluate with refinement means you'll make better decisions.
3. You **see themes and patterns**. By being able to identify connections between different aspects, you're more able to notice cause and effect. This opens up a whole new level of choices and opportunities, rather than being locked into a very limited repertoire of behaviours.

More consciousness leads to better decision-making – intuition becomes stronger

There's a lot of talk about how great it is to keep your options open. The idea is that more choice equates with more freedom. Actually, lots of choice is an uncomfortable state to be in. Not knowing what to do because you're faced with a constant stream of choices is exhausting.

What we actually want is to be choiceless. To be resolute. To be confident and clear. In any given moment you want to make the right decision. To know what is best in this moment. To recognise what is the obvious, right thing to be doing. To absolutely know the thing that will be best for you and everyone around you, in this moment, and for the future. That's the right action.

For this to happen you need to be more aware and perceptive. Being fully awake to all the possibilities allows you to make the right decision. And it shifts the decision-making process out of your head. Decision-making is not an intellectual process alone. It's a consciousness process. By being more conscious and less distracted, you can pick up on what's best in that moment.

Expansion of awareness leads you more in the direction of intuitively knowing what is best. Rather than simply relying on what you *think* is best, you're able to tune in to the deeper sense of what's right. You've removed the obstructions to accessing those subtle impulses.

This is why when someone learns to meditate, there are no required lifestyle changes or new rules of behaviour. What's right for one person may be totally different for another. It's about being able to tune in to what's right for *you*.

Here's how meditation helped one of my students get out of her head and tune in to something more subtle:

> *I believe the creative process can be divided into three stages: research and planning, at the beginning, plus the disciplined work of production to bring the project to life at the end. And in the middle there is a gap. This is the space where the idea germinates. Before I learned to meditate, my design strategy was to bridge that gap with my intellect. I tried to control every aspect of the process, not trusting my intuition, sense of wonder, or capacity for innovation. Meditation has given me the joy of going beyond thought, accessing a place of pure potential, where all ideas come from. I'm now able to trust that in between my research and production, I'll be able to detect that spark of inspiration which will become the seed of the idea for my design. This is the most successful and rewarding way to operate creatively in life.*

a word about:

Stepping into the Unknown

You should not be afraid of the unknown; it's actually the safe place. It is the ever-repeating known that smacks of stagnation, which always attracts scavengers.

Thom Knoles, Maharishi Vyasanand Saraswati

The great discoveries and insights of the world never happen when people stay within the confines of the current paradigm. In order to create the new, we have to let go of some of the old. This makes space for something more evolutionary and creative. Good ideas come from stepping out of the known into the unknown.

Fear is the biggest block to creativity. When you're afraid, it's much harder to let go. You're more likely to shore up the ever-repeating known, because that feels familiar and safe. This leads to a lot of effort and control to keep everything and everyone in line. 'If things (and people) stay just the way I need them to be, I'll be okay.'

When you let go of fear of change and evolution, you have a greater capacity to enthusiastically step into the unknown. Shake up the status quo and innovation happens.

Here Jessica, a very successful artist, describes how meditation has positively impacted her creativity:

Once I incorporated meditation into my daily life, my career as an artist jumped to another level. I began gravitating towards collaboration and community action, adding a new dimension of involvement with causes I believe in. Meditation propelled me to step into the unknown, taking risks in ways I hadn't before, which continues to be profoundly rewarding.

Also, in regards to my art-making process, meditation instilled a slowing down, an ability to sit with the unknown longer, resulting in my exploration of new twists and turns in my work as opposed to overworking or rushing a work to a known end. This increased ability to pause, step back and return to the source has proven to lead my work in a more authentic direction. Furthermore, meditation has fine-tuned my senses, increasing my ability to render more sensitively; refine the line quality in my drawing and detect greater subtleties in colour, tone and temperature.

Restful sleep

Restful sleep

It's very costly to be tired.

- No one makes their best decisions when they're worn out.
- Opportunities are missed when you're not alert and attentive.
- Accidents are far more likely when you're exhausted.
- You're more prone to arguments and misunderstandings when you haven't slept well.
- Physical and mental health is compromised when you're straining due to lack of rest.

Studies on sleep deprivation demonstrate clearly that we need sleep to function properly. Chronic sleep disturbance impairs your body's ability to function in a balanced way – cognitively, emotionally and physically. When someone is sleep-deprived their behaviour becomes more like someone who is drunk. Their speech is rambling and listless. It leads to irritability and crankiness. Taken to the extreme, if someone is kept awake for an extended period they become paranoid and even psychotic.

If you've had one bad night's sleep it won't hurt you. You'll probably feel a bit cranky and struggle to focus, but you'll make it through the day. It's when you consistently miss out on good sleep that things get more serious. When I teach a course I see it straight away. Most people are very tired. Insomnia is widespread. Students come in and after one or two meditations, the floodgates open. All the fatigue they've been carrying around for years starts to be released.

I remember a woman I taught who sat down at home on the sofa to meditate in the afternoon. It was day two of the course, so this was her third meditation in total. She meditated at about 5 p.m. and then lay down afterwards and woke up at 7.30 a.m. the next day! She couldn't remember sleeping so well, and so deeply, for decades.

Now you might be wondering why I'm talking about meditators feeling more tired. Isn't this meant to make you sleep better and have more energy? The reason it's common to feel tired in the early days is not because meditation is making you tired. Actually meditation is releasing the tiredness that's been stored in the system for years. Our bodies have a perfect accounting system when it comes to storing and tracking fatigue. It's all there, and it's been building up over time.

Meditation reveals the truth

Meditation will always reveal the truth of someone's experience. In this case, the true state of fatigue in the body is uncovered. We've all missed out on sleep, whether it be from working late, travelling, partying or being up all night with a sick child. The body stores that fatigue – layer upon layer. But along the way it becomes masked by the excitation stress chemistry in the system. This is what my friend and student Dr Nerina Ramlakhan refers to in her book *Tired But Wired: The Essential Sleep Toolkit*. I love this phrase, 'tired but wired', because it captures this state of being exhausted and yet at the same time operating on a cocktail of adrenaline and cortisol that allows us to push through the fog of fatigue. Human physiology is incredibly adaptable and even with insufficient sleep we can function, albeit suboptimally. However there's a high price to be paid.

Why good sleep matters

The impact of consistent, good-quality sleep improves our health and well-being in all sorts of ways:

- Your immune system will be stronger and more resilient. The inbuilt killer cells of the body are not compromised.
- You'll find it easier to stay slim. Sleep balances the hormones regulating hunger. The hormone leptin suppresses appetite and encourages the body to expend energy, while sleep deprivation reduces leptin. It's not surprising that we're seeing an increase in obesity alongside an epidemic of sleep disorders.
- You'll have more resistance to developing Type 2 diabetes. Studies have suggested that people who regularly sleep less than five hours a night have an increased risk of developing diabetes due to a reduction in glucose tolerance and insulin sensitivity.
- You'll prevent heart disease. Risk factors such as hypertension and increased heart rate have been shown to be negatively affected by short sleep duration. Hormones associated with systemic inflammation increase with disturbed and limited sleep.
- You reduce anxiety. We know anxiety can cause sleeping problems, and new research suggests sleep deprivation can lead to an anxiety disorder. Studies also show that people with chronic insomnia are at high risk of developing an anxiety disorder.
- You'll be in a better mood. It's a complex feedback loop because disrupted sleep can lead to emotional changes, including clinical depression, but these conditions can also disrupt sleep. It's well known that altered sleep patterns are a symptom of many mental health issues.

- You'll experience overall mental clarity. The brain's memory and learning centres are dependent on good sleep.

My student James shares how meditating has transformed his morning routine:

I was never a morning person, and always struggled with getting up. As we have a one-year-old, we decided to set our alarm early in order to meditate before the kids wake up. The alarm goes off at 6 a.m. and I'm now springing out of bed with genuine enthusiasm to get started. I love that I get to make a positive decision as the very first thing I do in the day. Starting on a positive note sets the tone for the whole day.

There's another benefit, which is significant for me personally. Pre-meditation, I would wake every morning with a slight feeling of anxiety in my stomach. I couldn't place what it was. It was nothing conscious on my mind but it had been there every morning for about two years. Since meditating, this has all but disappeared and I wake up without that feeling. It took a couple of months to go, but I'm pretty confident it's now a thing of the past.

How much sleep do you need?

We know that there are many factors that affect your sleep patterns, including life stage, seasonal changes, major stress triggers, lifestyle and underlying health conditions. The general guidelines for optimal sleep seem to fall somewhere between seven and nine hours every night.

I prefer to ask a slightly different question. How much *rest* do you need?

When you wake up in the morning do you feel energised and refreshed? How are your energy levels throughout the day – are you flagging by mid-afternoon or feeling okay? Are you falling asleep in front of the TV at 8 p.m. or are you able to stay awake and watch the whole show? Are you unable to get going until you've had one or two cups of coffee in the morning?

Before I learned to meditate my sleep was erratic and poor-quality. I was flying regularly for work, so I missed out on a lot of sleep with time-zone changes and long-haul flights. I was working long hours, so by the time I got home, had dinner and 'decompressed' from the day, I was going to bed pretty late. Exercise seemed to mask the tiredness because I'd get an energy boost after going for a run. I was often going out and having a few drinks and so I'd crash when I finally got into bed. I was dreaming a lot and I'm sure if you'd videoed me sleeping I would have been tossing and turning in a restless way. The bottom line – I was tired. My energy levels were not good even when I had slept what I thought was a reasonable number of hours.

Whatever's going on in your life will affect your energy levels and your ability to get good rest. Perhaps you have a long commute and your days are very long. Maybe you're recovering from an illness and going through treatments to help with that. Or you're taking medication with side effects that affect energy levels. Perhaps you have an elderly relative who needs a lot of care and that's falling on your shoulders. The list goes on.

Here's the experience from a student of how her sleep settled down and became more restful:

My dad died after a long illness about ten months before I learned to meditate. I've always had vivid dreams, but they were getting ridiculous – to the point where I wasn't sure sometimes when I woke up whether something had actually happened or it was a dream. And they were disturbing. Learning to meditate really calmed my dreams down and improved my sleep quality. I still have very lucid dreams, but they aren't disturbed like before and I don't wake up after eight hours of sleep feeling tired like I used to.

How meditation transforms sleep

Sleep plays a vital role in releasing stress and staying well. However, sleep alone doesn't provide enough rest to keep ahead of the game when it comes to stress release. Many people report a link between being stressed and unable to sleep. The thing they most need is not possible because they're in a hyper-excitatory state. This means they can't settle easily and falling asleep becomes an anxiety-inducing process in itself.

Pharmaceutical companies have flooded the market with medications to help people get to sleep – most of which are addictive and have negative side effects. And they don't work over the long term.

Pamela learned to meditate in her early sixties. Here's how meditation transformed her sleep:

Before learning to meditate I had the most horrible insomnia. I had tried everything – apps, devices, books and every lotion and potion available – all to no avail. Even more distressing, when I did fall asleep, I would wake with night terrors. My heart would be racing with fear. I had no idea what it was, but this pattern repeated most nights. I used to dread this happening as no matter what I did, I had no control over it. Since learning to meditate a year ago, I have not had one single night terror! This is simply astonishing. I'm sleeping the best I have for twenty years. This has been life-changing!

Again, rest is the antidote to stress

Meditation doesn't replace sleep, but it does have a direct and positive effect on the quality of those hours you spend lying around. The very deep rest of meditation each day takes the pressure off, so sleep can be restorative and revitalising. Meditators report being able to fall asleep more quickly and if they do wake up in the middle of the night, they're less anxious and more able to get back to sleep.

Meditation provides a different quality of rest than sleep

When you sleep your body is resting and your mind is dull. In meditation the body rests more deeply than sleep and yet the mind is alert, coherent and experiencing an inner state of bliss. It's a different quality of rest, where the mind–body is highly integrated. Rather than feeling the grogginess so common after sleep, the meditator finishes meditation more alert, deeply refreshed and ready for action.

Rhoda learned to meditate at the inspiring age of eighty-three, after many years of poor sleep:

My first, very noticeable and unexpected benefit was sleep. For many years, my sleep patterns were erratic – I didn't sleep for more than three hours at a time. Soon after starting to meditate, I began to sleep between six and eight hours a night. Not every night, but more often than not.

a word about:

When to Sleep

Perhaps you heard your grandmother say something like, 'The hours before midnight are worth twice those after.' Ayurveda, the Vedic system of healthcare, agrees with Grandma. When you sleep is one of the most important factors in improving your energy levels. And aligning your sleep patterns to the rhythm of nature has benefits for all aspects of your mental and physical health.

Ayurveda recognises that the qualities of early morning are very different to those of the middle of the night. When we align ourselves with nature, we'll sleep better and feel more energetic and happier.

The recommendation is to wake early, around 6 a.m., when the qualities of lightness and movement are dominant. Waking at this time means you carry those feelings of alertness and energy into your day.

You may be panicking at the idea of waking at 6 a.m. The key is to get to bed earlier. Have you noticed around 9.30 p.m., you start to flag and feel sleepy? This is the night-time phase, where the qualities of heaviness and calm are conducive to more restful sleep. Let's say you ignore that sleepy feeling because you've got work to do, emails to write and something to watch on TV. Now it's midnight and you're wide awake and a bit hungry. You've moved into a phase characterised by increased energy and focus, making it harder to nod off.

Also, this is an important time to be resting so vital metabolic and healing processes can happen. Going to bed around 10 p.m. makes it easier to fall asleep, and reduces the likelihood of food cravings. This positively impacts weight loss and, interestingly, skin problems may also improve if you get to bed earlier.

I know many people who say they're not a morning person and they're most creative late at night. Almost always they're staying up very late and then sleeping in late, which means they feel slow and sluggish all morning. When they start getting up earlier, they're ready to fall asleep at night. They gain more energy overall and often need less sleep.

My recommendation is to take it slowly. Gradually adjust your schedule every few days, in the direction of an earlier bedtime, rather than going cold turkey and shocking your system into a very different routine too quickly.

reason to meditate #8

Slower ageing

Slower ageing

When we think of getting older we naturally mean how many birthdays we've had. Using chronological age is the normal way people determine how old they are. Yet basing age on how many times the Earth has gone round the sun is a pretty limited way of looking at the rate at which someone is ageing. Everyone ages differently. We all know people who seem youthful and dynamic well into their seventies and eighties, and then others who at fifty have the air of someone decades older.

I remember a man in his early forties who came to learn to meditate. He had a very demanding role in finance in the City of London, and a young family who he didn't see very much. He had a long commute to a job he didn't really like. He explained he felt trapped because he was very well paid and had a lot of expenses, including private school fees and a big mortgage. He wasn't sleeping well, drank alcohol most nights to unwind, had no time for exercise and was feeling anxious and unhappy. He'd recently been for a physical check-up and was put on blood pressure medication, told to lose 10 kg and to reduce his stress levels.

It was a wake-up call. His father had died relatively young from a heart attack, and he was terrified he was heading down the same path. He'd read about some top hedge fund manager who credited meditation for his success and he thought he'd check it out.

Biological age vs chronological age

While some of this man's situation may be down to genetics, the largest factor was how he was living his life. Poor sleep, unhealthy diet, lack of exercise, high stress levels and lack of job satisfaction were all creating a fast-track to rapid ageing. Even though his chronological age was only forty-three, I'm sure his biological age was much older.

The *Adult Growth Examination* (AGE) was developed by Robert Morgan in 1968 to provide a standardised test determining the rate at which someone is ageing. By measuring three primary markers of hearing, near-point vision and systolic blood pressure, a simple, reliable test of someone's biological age was devised.

When AGE is applied in studies, it shows clearly that meditation slows down the ageing process. One study compared meditators to an extensive body of data collected by the US Public Health Service. Long-term meditators (those who had been meditating for five years or more) were an average of twelve years younger than their chronological age. Not surprisingly, how long someone had been meditating impacted the results. Yet even those who had been meditating for less than five years had a lower biological age – around five years less than their chronological age.

Stress leads to premature ageing

It makes sense that if you're calmer and more adaptable you're going to be less stressed. The knock-on effect is that with less wear and tear on the body and less disturbance of the mind, you will not age as quickly.

In meditation, as thinking becomes more quiet, the body rests. As the mind continues to settle, the body becomes even more restful. Then a point comes when the activity of the mind is so refined it's almost imperceptible and finally the thoughts go.

The mind falls mute. In this state of least-excitation the metabolic rate has nearly reached zero. By regularly experiencing this ground state, the meditator counterbalances the wear and tear of daily life. This twice-daily experience allows the nervous system to recharge, renew and repair. The ageing process slows down.

DHEA-S – the hormone of longevity

We've discussed the changes in hormonal balance that affect our mood and health. When it comes to ageing, there are many hormones that play a part. One stand-out biomarker of ageing is *dehydroepiandrosterone sulphate* (DHEA-S). This hormone, found in the adrenal glands, is at its highest level when you're a young adult and then declines as you age. Higher levels of DHEA-S have been associated with a stronger immune system, less heart disease, greater bone density and longevity. Low levels of DHEA-S in women have been linked to breast cancer.

A 1980s study of middle-aged and older meditators showed that they maintained higher levels of DHEA-S than a non-meditating control group. In fact DHEA-S levels in the meditators were on a par with levels of non-meditators five to ten years younger. This is exciting because it shows that, rather than relying on drugs and artificial means, we have the capacity to retard the premature ageing process naturally, by normalising the delicate hormonal balance from within.

a word about:

Free Radicals

No discussion about ageing would be complete without considering the destructive effect of free radicals.

Free radicals are small, highly reactive molecules, usually derived from oxygen. They are short one electron and this imbalance creates an insatiable appetite to abduct neighbouring electrons to resolve their own instability. When the body is well and in balance, we have the enzymes to neutralise these molecular scavengers. However when free radicals are created too quickly for the body to handle they take over, causing the destruction of nearby cells and undermining the body's natural repair mechanisms. Common factors that speed up the creation of free radicals are: alcohol, tobacco smoke, highly processed foods, certain drugs, pesticides, air pollution, overexposure to the sun, chemotherapy and stress.

Dr Hari Sharma is an expert in this field. In his book Freedom from Disease *he says: 'Most researchers studying free radicals estimate that these deadly molecules help to cause 80 to 90 per cent of the degenerative diseases that afflict the human race.'*

Research shows that free radicals are linked to almost all chronic diseases including cancer, heart disease, strokes, arteriosclerosis, emphysema, rheumatoid arthritis, Crohn's disease and diabetes, as well as speeding up the ageing process itself.

The good news is there's a lot we can do to strengthen our inbuilt defence mechanisms and soak up excess free radicals. Diet is a big factor here – particularly increasing antioxidant-rich foods like whole grains, fresh fruit and vegetables. The natural phytochemicals in fresh vegetables support your body at the chemical level. And when you combine these veggies with turmeric, you're really maximising the anti-inflammatory and anti-cancer effects of the phytochemicals.

Good sleep helps keep free radicals at bay and, as we've just seen, getting good-quality sleep is vital for many reasons.

However, the most powerful way to deal with these 'molecular sharks' is to reduce your stress levels, because stress produces free radicals en masse. This brings us full circle to meditation. As we've seen, the stress-busting powers of meditation are huge. One study showed that free radical activity was 27 per cent lower among meditators. By minimising your stress levels with meditation, you have a powerful tool to stop free radicals before they start wreaking havoc.

With age comes wisdom

Evidence shows that as a meditator, not only are you adding years to your life, the quality and richness of those years is also improved. Physically you're healthier and stronger, and mentally and emotionally you're more balanced and happier.

Equally importantly, your attitude to ageing changes. Rather than resisting the process and trying to artificially slow it down, there's a sense that life is becoming more meaningful. When a sense of self-awareness is becoming more stable, you're more confident in yourself. There's a growing capacity to trust your own, inner sense of what feels right. Access to a broader state of consciousness delivers a more expansive view of life. You gain more perspective and understanding.

Rather than living a life by trial and error and learning from mistakes, this expanded awareness means we don't try to reinvent the wheel with every decision we face. And so with age, comes wisdom.

Chay learned to meditate when he was sixty-eight, two months after retiring:

> It was only when I retired that I seriously began to look for a course on meditation. How much less stressful my working life could have been if I had learned earlier. After forty-five years of full-time work, stepping away from the controlled patterns that had imposed was not a comfortable feeling. Learning meditation has been a real boon in helping me to comfortably adjust to my changed circumstances at this stage in my life.
>
> One of the big improvements is learning to listen to, and trust, my inner feelings more than my logical thought. My daily interactions with people are much more pleasant. I feel more rested and less fatigued. I definitely feel more content and much less apprehensive.

Fulfilling relationships

Fulfilling relationships

When you're healthier, happier, energised and conscious, you're a nicer person to be around. When you're unwell, feeling down, stressed and exhausted, you're not available for others in a way that is uplifting. Quite simply, how you feel and behave affects every relationship and social interaction you have.

At some deep level we know this. We're social creatures – interdependence is a fundamental feature of human life. We all live in community to some degree. The word community originates from the Latin *communis*, which means common. Our common needs for survival and fulfilment run deep. Social interactions and relationships go to the heart of how we meet these common goals.

Fundamental principles of relating

Relationships are based on *giving*. If you're happier, more fulfilled and more aware, your contribution to social interactions is high-grade. This will positively impact everyone who is in your orbit. And if you give something of value it will come back to you many times over.

Reciprocity is fundamental in relationships. The old saying 'As you sow, so shall you reap' sums this up beautifully. What you give will come back to you. If you want kindness, give kindness. If you want attention, give attention. And the reverse is true. If you bring neediness and tension to a relationship, don't be surprised by what you get back.

Relationships are like a *third entity* – they have a personality that reflects what is being fed to them. Just like a thirsty plant responds to regular water and sunshine, a relationship is nourished by what you bring to it. If you contribute nourishing attention, your relationships grow and flourish. If you ignore them or give them the wrong kind of attention, they'll wither and die.

How consciousness affects relationships

As we've been discovering, consciousness is the basis of life. The degree to which you are conscious or aware impacts every thought and action you take. This directly and significantly impacts the quality of your relationships. Here's a simple flow chart to demonstrate how this works:

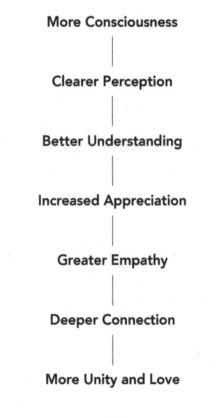

More Consciousness

|

Clearer Perception

|

Better Understanding

|

Increased Appreciation

|

Greater Empathy

|

Deeper Connection

|

More Unity and Love

Let's analyse this. The more conscious you are, the more information you're able to take in which means you're more able to perceive what's going on around you. This expanded awareness also allows you to perceive things more clearly and accurately. As a result, the ability to form a view about the best set of responses at any given moment will grow.

The more clearly you're able to perceive the reality of a situation, the more understanding you have about why someone is behaving in a certain way. If you lack understanding you lose the context through which to interpret what's going on.

Understanding fosters appreciation. By being able to see what's causing a person to behave in a particular way, you're better able to appreciate them and empathise with what it's like to be in their shoes. You're more able to see what it's like for the other person: 'If I had to deal with everything that person has to deal with, I'd probably behave in the same way.'

When we clearly attune ourselves to what someone else is feeling, then we're able to connect on a deeper level. And with connection we're able to experience unity – the coming together in a shared experience. This is the basis of a truly loving and kind relationship.

Vivian came to meditation with the main aim of improving her relationships. Here's her experience:

Relationship troubles were what brought me to meditation. I thought my marriage was on the rocks, my relationship with my children was very poor and more than half my friends were not the ones my mum would approve of. Slowly and consistently, I managed to get out of most of the toxic relationships, and decided for myself which relationships I wanted to put my energy into. The results were incredible. My marriage situation is no longer the biggest problem in my life, my children became my priority again and I'm able to say no to some people who once had a massive hold on me. I couldn't have done it without meditation.

How stress affects relationships

Stress makes you do the opposite of what's needed in social relationships. You offer acceptance when what's needed is a firm hand. Or you discipline someone when they simply need to be listened to. You're disengaged when you should be attentive. You're pushy when you should be more tolerant.

Also when we're stressed we may have low self-worth and accept appalling behaviour. We try to adapt, when actually we should be making a stand for our deserving power.

When we're stressed and someone is offering us something lovely, we don't see it and so we reject it and miss the opportunity for connection. Stress ends up blinding us to what is the correct response.

Here's a very honest example of one student's relationship with her children since meditating:

I'm more patient with my children and I love that. I very rarely shout at them as I'm able to internalise my frustration and make sense of it, rather than taking it out on a little person who is maybe going through their own thing, and needs an understanding mummy rather than a shouty mummy. I remember dropping a packet of peas all over the floor shortly after learning to meditate, and swearing rather loudly. My daughter said to me, 'Mummy I don't think your meditation is working today or did you forget to do it?' So clearly she noticed a change too! One thing that

people often say is how calm and well-behaved my children are.
I really think meditation has helped me to facilitate that in them.

Be the uplifting one

There's a basic principle in life – what you put your attention on, grows.

Imagine a gardener looking at all her plants. In her hand is a hose with the water running. She turns to look at some weeds. 'Oh no! Where have these come from? Look how fast they are growing! They're crowding out the flowers!' As she stands and complains, water is flowing. She's watering the weeds. Not surprisingly, they grow even faster and take over the garden.

Similarly, whatever you put your attention on is enlivened. When you attend to something or someone, there's a flow of energy and intelligence. Sanskrit has a beautiful word for this – *Soma*.

Soma is expressive of the flow of consciousness. When you put your attention on someone, your soma flows to them.

Just like the gardener watering her plants, your soma tap is always flowing. Water the weeds, and they will grow. Water the flowers, and they flourish. So when you meet someone, notice where your awareness goes. If you focus on their flaws, those imperfections magnify. Put your attention on the person's finer qualities, and those grow and expand.

You don't even have to be physically present for the same dynamic to occur. If you're constantly thinking about a situation or person that you don't enjoy, your soma flows to them. As a result, negativity will grow until it dominates your thinking.

171

Whatever you put your attention on in life expands. Make a decision to pay attention to what you want to become stronger in your life. Let go and stop watering what you wish to fall away.

a word about:

Unrealistic Views of Others

Often trouble arises in relationships when we're not getting what we want. 'I want more attention.' 'I want more kindness.' 'I want more personal space.' We have to understand that it's not possible to control what other people can give us. But we can control what we give. So rather than attempting to control others in order to get more, we need to look at how to be better givers.

We also need to develop a more realistic view of what we're likely to receive. It doesn't serve us or the relationship if we develop mistaken expectations and get ourselves upset because we were expecting something that was never going to come from that person.

As a wise man once said: 'Don't water a walnut tree and expect to harvest mangoes. It's not the fault of the tree – walnut trees don't produce mangoes. It's a shame to be surprised when a walnut tree delivers walnuts.' If you get surprised and upset because you're not getting what you want, it may be a lack of perception about what kind of tree you're sitting under.

More peace in the world

More peace in the world

You don't need to look very hard to see we're living in a world filled with suffering. On page one of your news feed you'll see things like corporate malfeasance, crime, illness, oppression, brutality, hardship, political corruption, racism and climate crisis.

Understandably, many people feel helpless and overwhelmed by the scale of the challenges we face. It's tempting to just opt out – 'It's all too much. What difference could I possibly make?' As a result people shut down and go small in their thinking about what's possible. It feels easier to wait for others to step up and take action.

When people are tired and stressed, they don't have the energy to engage. They can't see clearly. They don't have the broad-spectrum awareness of what's going on, so they become increasingly gullible and narrow. Overwhelmed and lacking self-confidence, they become fearful of the unknown and less able to take action.

How do we change these deep, systemic problems in the collective? We start with ourselves.

Peaceful people make a peaceful society

The individual is the base unit of any group. Nations, cities, companies, schools, families – all are a composite of individuals. Like a living organism, the health of a group depends upon the health of its individual parts. The state of consciousness of each person shapes the broader group they belong to.

If you want the forest to be lush and green, you need green, healthy trees. If the forest is full of brown, stressed, dead trees, then the whole forest is affected. When the individuals of a society are happier, healthier and more creative, society will be uplifted, balanced and innovative.

It's the few who lead the many

It always has been. Change doesn't come from the top down. It's a bottom-up process. It starts with each and every one of us. All the great change-makers in the world were individuals who were willing to step out of the ever-repeating known. Rather than being hypnotised by the social conditioning of the time, they were willing to shake things up and challenge the status quo. Sometimes the existing state of affairs is so deeply ingrained, and baked into the systems and laws, that it demands a huge effort to shift. When Mahatma Gandhi stood up to the entrenched injustices of colonialism, it took monumental levels of unbending intent to continue forward. His example pulled others into his orbit, the one became a few, and then the few became the many. It's always one brave person who instigates this cascade of change.

People behave according to their state of consciousness

As is a person's level of consciousness, then that's how they behave. No amount of coercing, shaming or lecturing will change someone. When people behave in ways that are not socially acceptable, it's not based on a lack of information about what's right. This is why more laws and more enforcement won't fundamentally change things for the good. What will change the current situation is something, anything, that increases people's level of consciousness.

What's your personal peace balance?

What can you do today (and every day) that supports your evolution and those around you? At the end of the day, are you a giver of peace and adaptability, or are you a giver of stress and neediness? This is where meditation shifts your personal balance. More and more, you end up sharing that which is valuable, rather than adding to the collective in a way that is neither progressive or smooth.

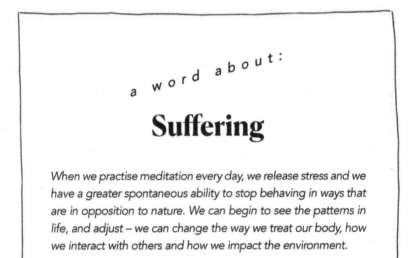

a word about:

Suffering

When we practise meditation every day, we release stress and we have a greater spontaneous ability to stop behaving in ways that are in opposition to nature. We can begin to see the patterns in life, and adjust – we can change the way we treat our body, how we interact with others and how we impact the environment.

When you're stressed, it's more likely you'll be at odds with the world around you and this leads to suffering. If someone goes against nature, whether consciously or not, a correction occurs. A toddler playing with a power socket will get some correction. Even without him understanding, Mum will have her way and pull him out of danger. Mum's correction is a way of stopping her child from suffering. If he ignores the correction, he'll suffer.

The more prolonged the ignoring, the more intense the suffering. Continuing to make 'mistakes' about the best course of action will ramp up the correction to a point where it can feel very rough. And suffering will always involve others. You cannot suffer in isolation. It will drag others along with you and it will spread – into your family, your workplace, your society.

> Because we live in a world that's habituated to reinventing the wheel and learning by trial and error, there's a common misconception that repeatedly making mistakes is part and parcel of learning.
>
> I disagree. We don't need to reinvent the wheel. We need to get better at detecting what's going on. The way to do this is to quieten down your mind and body and keep the distortions (stress) to a minimum, so you're more in tune with what's happening. Then you make mistakes less frequently and suffering goes down.

The need of the time

I'd like to come back to what I said at the beginning:

Meditation, when done properly, works. It isn't weird. Scientific evidence backs it up. Anyone can do it. It will positively change the way you feel and perform.

I write this based on my personal experience and the experiences of thousands of students. My motivation to change career and become a teacher of meditation was because of the impact it had on my life in a short space of time. And my motivation in writing this book has been to share that knowledge so we can have informed conversations about ways to bring about positive change.

The need of the time demands that we look at what works and what doesn't work. The unsustainability of the current approach to living is evident. At the macro level it's obvious. Nature is shouting at us, yet as a species we continue on, enabling more and more destruction of the planet. Tension, conflict and even wars abound between nations. At an individual level, the same struggles and strains play out. The health of the planet, and the people who live on it, is in a precarious state.

We don't need more people telling us how to behave. We need more people living their lives as an example of something good and inspiring. Just as negativity spreads, so does positivity.

Someone who feels good inside themselves has a look about them. A sense of friendliness and calm; and an air of confidence radiates from them. In challenging situations they have the ability to respond with behaviour that's helpful. They spontaneously behave in a way that is not needy. They contribute to the collective in ways that are uplifting and they draw people to them.

Most people are dumping stress all over those around them. When we meditate we release our stresses in a socially responsible manner. Our practice doesn't require the participation of others. Rather than releasing stress in a way that involves others and pollutes society, we self-purify and then engage with others in a more graceful way.

When someone decides not to learn to meditate, I say, 'Fine. And if not this, then what?' What are you doing that's going to give you energy and help you sleep naturally? What is your strategy to stay mentally and physically healthy? How are you releasing stress chemistry from your system? What are your plans for upgrading your relationships and feeling more joy in your life?

I'm not suggesting meditation is the only thing that works. There are many ways we can change our lives for the better, and change we must – the current paradigm isn't working. If not meditation, then I encourage you to find something that will address these issues in a way that's good for you, and everyone around you.

Why meditate? Because it works.

RESOURCES

Jillian was trained to teach Vedic Meditation by Thom Knoles, Maharishi Vyasanand Saraswati. Thom trained as a teacher of Transcendental Meditation (TM) with Maharishi Mahesh Yogi. He then taught for over twenty-five years with groups affiliated with Maharishi.

Thom now teaches independently of the TM organisations. He continues to teach meditation as he learned from Maharishi. Jillian teaches in just the same way.

Jillian is an independent teacher of Vedic Meditation. She is not affiliated with the Transcendental Meditation organisations. Services, processes and programmes may differ.

Jillian's approach to teaching

I teach an automatic self-transcending technique of meditation called Vedic Meditation. My commitment is to teach in the purity of the Vedic tradition, as I was shown by my teacher and he was by his teacher. I'm an independent instructor and am not connected to any organisation.

Learning to meditate involves taking an in-person course, over four consecutive days. Each session is about two hours. Once you've taken the course you know how to meditate properly and you're off and running. You have a powerful tool to use every day for the rest of your life. There's also lots of support and guidance along the way, as your experiences develop and deepen.

Here's the structure of the course:

Day 1: *You're instructed in your mantra and taught the basics of how to meditate. No messing around.*

Day 2: *Building on the previous session, we discuss your experiences and give you guidance to fit meditation into your busy life.*

Day 3: *You gain a deep understanding of how meditation releases stress and how this relates to what's happening in your meditation.*

Day 4: *We look at the road ahead. Meditation fundamentally upgrades your life and we discuss what this looks like.*

The course works because it gives you *complete* knowledge – both experiential and theoretical understanding. I could talk and write about meditation for a long time, but until you get a taste of it for yourself, you don't have complete knowledge. This is why we get you meditating on the first day and then build on your personal experiences.

You can contact me here:
@jillianlavender
@londonmeditationcentre
www.LondonMeditationCentre.com
www.NewYorkMeditationCenter.com

Finding a meditation teacher

Connecting with a skilled teacher is a vital part of your meditation journey. There are many teachers around the world who are teaching an automatic self-transcending style of meditation and a quick web search will turn up instructors near you. Learning to meditate is an important life skill, so I recommend finding someone who is teaching with integrity and care.

What to consider when choosing a teacher:

- Is this someone with whom you resonate?
- Are they inspiring and trustworthy?
- Can they answer your questions in a full and meaningful way?
- Do they communicate in a timely and professional way?
- Is there an opportunity to ask questions in a live format?
- Did they learn this knowledge from a successful and professional teacher with a proven track record?
- Are they offering ongoing support as your meditation journey develops?
- Do they teach in person?
- Do they have students they can connect you with in order to gain more perspective?

Websites:

Jillian's websites are below and also that of her teacher, Vedic master Thom Knoles (Maharishi Vyasanand Saraswati).
JillianLavender.com
LondonMeditationCentre.com
NewYorkMeditationCenter.com
ThomKnoles.com

Books I've referenced and others I like:

Vedic knowledge

The Upanishads, by Alistair Shearer (with Peter Russell)

The Yoga Sutras of Patanjali, translated by Alistair Shearer

Stress

Stress Without Distress, by Hans Selye

When the Body Says No, by Gabor Maté

Stress, a Brief History, by Cary L. Cooper and Philip Dewe

Brain, Science and Consciousness

The XX Brain, by Dr Lisa Mosconi

Waking Up in Time, by Peter Russell

Creating Affluence, by Deepak Chopra

Molecules of Emotion, by Candace Pert PhD

The Tao of Physics: An Exploration of the Parallels between Modern Physics and Eastern Mysticism, by Fritjof Capra

Ayurveda and Health

A Woman's Best Medicine, by Nancy Lonsdorf M.D., Veronica Butler M.D., Melanie Brown PhD

Freedom from Disease, by Dr Hari Sharma

Sleep

Tired but Wired, by Dr Nerina Ramlakhan

Sleep Recovery: The Five Step Yoga Solution to Restore Your Rest, by Lisa Sanfilippo

Acknowledgements

I've been wanting to write this book for many years. The fact that it's finally happened is down to many people.

One of the biggest reasons *Why Meditate?* has come together is due to the thousands of students I've taught over nearly twenty years. Without students, there is no teacher. They are the ones who helped me consolidate my understanding and develop my delivery of this knowledge. They are constant reminders of how powerful and necessary this technique of meditation is. Thank you to everyone who has been open and willing to place their trust in me as they embark on their meditation journey.

The team at Yellow Kite have been incredibly supportive. Thank you to Liz Gough for reaching out in the beginning, and a special thanks to my editor Carolyn Thorne for guiding me and trusting me to get my ideas and vision on paper. Thanks to Liv Nightingall for assisting along the way. I'm also grateful to Jacqui Lewis for making the editing process smooth and efficient.

My vision for this project has been to reflect what I teach. Therefore, not only must the words be clear and inspiring, I also wanted the book to feel modern and accessible. This wouldn't have happened without the involvement of some very talented women. As I began to write, Tamara Adlin gave me great advice and very practical help with the process itself. Huge thanks to my friend and colleague Marisa Lowenstein for her patience and talent as we fine-tuned her very cool illustrations. And a big thank you to Karin Ludwig and Anna Liebau at elle+elle for their refined and brilliant design talent.

Many people contributed content to make this knowledge come alive and inspire others. Thank you to all the students who shared their stories of how Vedic Meditation has transformed their lives – hearing it straight from them adds so much to the message of this book. Thank you to my friend and student, Sophie Dear for sharing her expertise of a powerful breathing technique to help with moments of stress. Many, many thanks to Eric Braun for his continued wise and trusted counsel. A special thanks to my dear friend, Jeff Seroy for taking the time to read my manuscript and for his generous and expert advice over the many years that I was thinking about the book. I'm also grateful to Alistair Shearer for allowing me to share some of his work as a master of Sanskrit and Vedic knowledge. My ability to teach is directly linked to my own teacher, Thom Knoles, Maharishi Vyasanand Saraswati. I met Thom over two decades ago back in Jersey Road, Sydney and it was truly a 'fork in the road' moment. Due to his inspiration I learned to meditate and then many years later had the great good fortune to train with him one-on-one to become a teacher myself. I am forever grateful to have learned from a master and custodian of the Vedic knowledge of the highest level.

And finally, much closer to home, a huge thank you to Emma Rae who is a key part of the team at London and New York Meditation Centres. Emma helped me on so many levels – enthusiastic, ready to step up, and always being there with practical and emotional support.

And last of all my family. Thank you to my dear partner Michael and our darling daughter, Loie. This book is for you both and because of you both. Loie, thank you for being so patient with mama taking so much of our family time to write. And Michael – without you this book wouldn't have happened. Thank you for listening (and listening) and editing and suggesting and sense-checking. Most importantly thank you for caring and cheering for me every step of the way. Love and Jai Guru Deva.